ATLAS OF
STUDENT
MOBILITY

Published by the Institute of International Education with grant support from the Ford Foundation

Institute of International Education
809 United Nations Plaza
New York, NY 10017

Todd M. Davis
Senior Scholar

Renée Meyer
Layout and Graphic Design

Marie O'Sullivan
Editorial Support

ISBN 0-87206-272-4

CONTENTS

FEATURES OF THIS ATLAS 6

The Atlas of Student Mobility

THE ATLAS PROJECT

Attendees at the 16th annual Australian International Education Conference were startled when Anthony Bohem, with IDP Education Australia, presented the results of a groundbreaking report that projected the growth in demand for an international education by students worldwide. His thesis was straightforward. As developing nations become wealthier and as their population increases, the number of students that potentially will go abroad may double before 2015 and double again by 2025. In 2000 UNESCO estimated that over 1.7 million students are currently being educated at the tertiary level in countries other than their homes and the IDP report predicted that by 2025 almost eight million students will be educated trans-nationally.

While the numbers of international students are likely to grow, so will the complexity of their mobility patterns. For example, in the recent past, as the Southeast Asian Tiger economies have matured, the field of study choices of internationally minded students from these places has broadened to include undergraduate students in the humanities, as well as graduate students in the engineering disciplines. For example, mobility patterns now include significant intra-regional movement, as well as the more traditional pattern of movement from the developing world to Western Europe and the United States. For example, during 1995, intra-Asian mobility constituted over 18% of the 687,000 internationally mobile Asian students. Similarly about 17% of South American students seeking an international educational experience do so in other South American universities, as reported by UNESCO. International education trends and patterns should be looked at in relation to other international flows as well as national developments such as the home country investment in human capital, population growth, the level of technological capacity, the growth of civil liberty, and international connectedness. It is in the context of these larger shifts that international mobility occurs and in this sense global mobility is a component of an emerging world-system of exchanges that began to evolve since the end of the Cold War.

Unfortunately we don't have anything like the complete picture about global mobility. What is lacking is a source of baseline data that enables us to see this emerging world higher education space as more than the sum of its national host country parts. With Ford Foundation support, the Institute of International Education is working closely with its partners, the British Council and IDP Education Australia, and others to create a global focus on international student mobility. Currently, national level planners tend to be bounded in their planning by national borders. By creating a shared image of international mobility, we hope to highlight the truly globe-spanning aspects of higher education, make apparent the emerging world higher education economy, and establish a conversation space for those concerned with global education mobility issues. This atlas of global student mobility is one means to achieve these ends.

FEATURES OF THIS ATLAS
21 leading global destinations, listed alphabetically

Introductory text panel places a country's international student population in context. The panel points the reader to important characteristics of its international enrollments.

The national flag for these leading hosts is displayed.

A detailed close-up map points the reader to the area of greatest concentration of international students for a particular host.

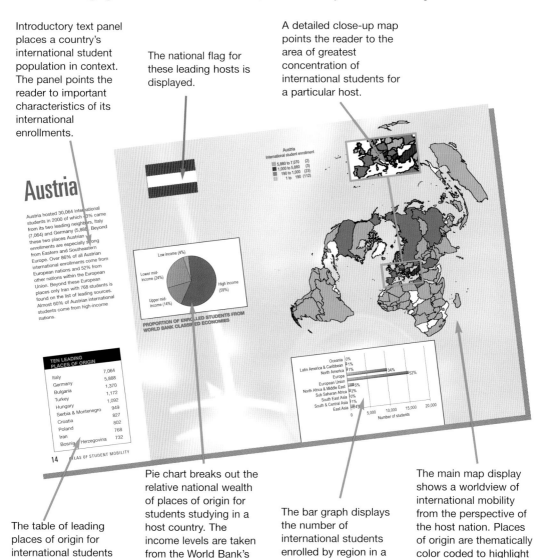

Austria
International student enrollment
5,880 to 7,070 (2)
1,000 to 5,880 (3)
190 to 1,000 (23)
1 to 190 (112)

Austria

Austria hosted 30,064 international students in 2000 of which 43% came from its two leading neighbors, Italy (7,064) and Germany (5,888). Beyond these two places Austrian enrollments are especially strong from Eastern and Southeastern Europe. Over 86% of all Austrian international enrollments come from European nations and 52% from other nations within the European Union. Beyond these European places only Iran with 768 students is found on the list of leading sources. Almost 60% of Austrian international students come from high-income nations.

Low income (4%)

Lower mid-income (24%)

High income (59%)

Upper mid-income (14%)

PROPORTION OF ENROLLED STUDENTS FROM WORLD BANK CLASSIFIED ECONOMIES

TEN LEADING PLACES OF ORIGIN

Italy	7,064
Germany	5,888
Bulgaria	1,370
Turkey	1,172
Hungary	1,092
Serbia & Montenegro	949
Croatia	827
Poland	802
Iran	768
Bosnia Herzegovina	732

14 ATLAS OF STUDENT MOBILITY

Oceania 0%
Latin America & Caribbean 1%
North America 1%
Europa
European Union 34% 52%
North Africa & Middle East 5%
Sub Saharan Africa 2%
South East Asia 0%
South & Central Asia 1%
East Asia 4%
0   5,000   10,000   15,000   20,000
Number of students

The table of leading places of origin for international students studying in a host nation lists in convenient rank order the ten leading origins.

Pie chart breaks out the relative national wealth of places of origin for students studying in a host country. The income levels are taken from the World Bank's classification system and provide an insight into features of the origin places related to national wealth.

The bar graph displays the number of international students enrolled by region in a particular host. This graph provides a quick reference to the geographic reach of a host nation.

The main map display shows a worldview of international mobility from the perspective of the host nation. Places of origin are thematically color coded to highlight particularly important places of origin.

75 leading global places of origin

The 75 most important places of origin for internationally mobile students are presented within their World Bank classification categories and listed in order of the number of students from these places who are studying in other countries.

The relative wealth, government form and dominant religion give insight into the national, historical and cultural context within which international mobility occurs.

Every effort has been made to ensure that the national flag for these places is accurate and up-to-date.

The percent of students abroad who are studying in the European Union, an English speaking destination and as a percent of all higher education students is displayed.

For each place of origin, details of its higher education system and the number of its nationals seeking an education abroad is displayed.

Tabled data shows the leading destination countries for internationally mobile students coming from a particular place of origin.

Pie chart displays in graphic form the destination countries for students from a particular place of origin.

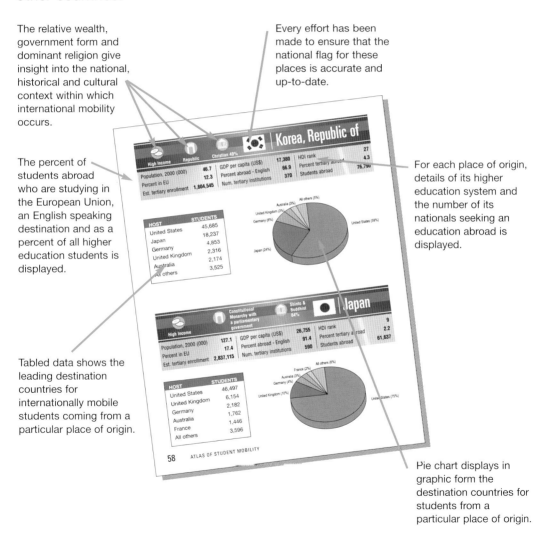

DESTINATION

In 2002 there were 89 free countries in which there is broad scope for open political competition, a climate of respect for civil liberties, significant independent civic life, and independent media. This represents 2.718 billion people and 43.85 percent of the global population.

Source: Freedom House

Reflection: All people have inalienable rights to life, liberty and property, including intellectual property, by virtue of being born free and equal and are equally endowed with the right to access education including, international education, on the basis of merit.

Principle 1 Halkidiki Declaration

21 DESTINATIONS

These figures, read by column, show the total international enrollments for 21 leading hosts for whom data was available and which are included in this atlas. The significance of these enrollments for destinations is not easily summed into a single simple figure. Rather, these enrollment patterns represent long standing geopolitical, linguistic and historical relationships between destination and origin places. The movement of students across national frontiers represents but one form of exchange. It is of note that the two leading destinations account for over half of the student mobility included in this atlas and the leading five hosts account for over three quarters of all international student mobility, as of 2000-2001.

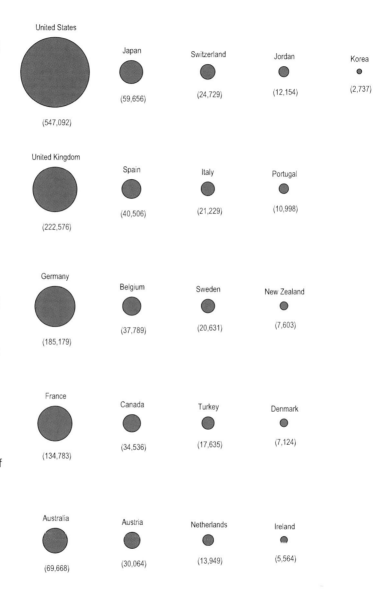

United States
(547,092)

Japan
(59,656)

Switzerland
(24,729)

Jordan
(12,154)

Korea
(2,737)

United Kingdom
(222,576)

Spain
(40,506)

Italy
(21,229)

Portugal
(10,998)

Germany
(185,179)

Belgium
(37,789)

Sweden
(20,631)

New Zealand
(7,603)

France
(134,783)

Canada
(34,536)

Turkey
(17,635)

Denmark
(7,124)

Australia
(69,668)

Austria
(30,064)

Netherlands
(13,949)

Ireland
(5,564)

Australia

Australia hosts almost 70,000 international higher education students onshore and is the fifth largest host worldwide. A leader in transnational education, Australia also enrolls 34,000 students in offshore programs. While Australia is a global player, its onshore enrollments have a distinctly regional flavor. Almost 50% of Australia's enrollments come from Southeast Asia: notably Malaysia (9,866), Indonesia (9,283) and Singapore (8,647). Beyond this area Australia also draws heavily on students from elsewhere in Asia. Nearly three-quarters of all Australian enrollments come from Asia. A notable exception is the United States. The United States is the only nation outside of Asia among the ten largest places of origin for international students in Australia.

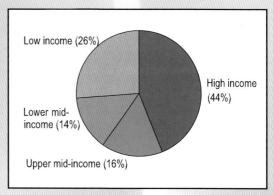

PROPORTION OF ENROLLED STUDENTS FROM WORLD BANK CLASSIFIED ECONOMIES

TEN LEADING PLACES OF ORIGIN	
Malaysia	9,866
Indonesia	9,283
Singapore	8,647
Hong Kong	6,502
India	4,374
China	3,712
United States	2,846
Thailand	2,716
Taiwan	2,440
Korea, Republic of	2,174

Note: The destination maps were created using an azmuthal equidistant projection. These maps are scaled at 1″ to 2,775 miles. All projections of the earth contain distortions, some of area others of distance, shape or direction. The projection system chosen for this atlas is especially good at representing large, continent and ocean sized objects and preserve direction from the center point allowing distortions in both area and shape. These projections allow the viewer the opportunity to reflect on global student mobility in new ways.

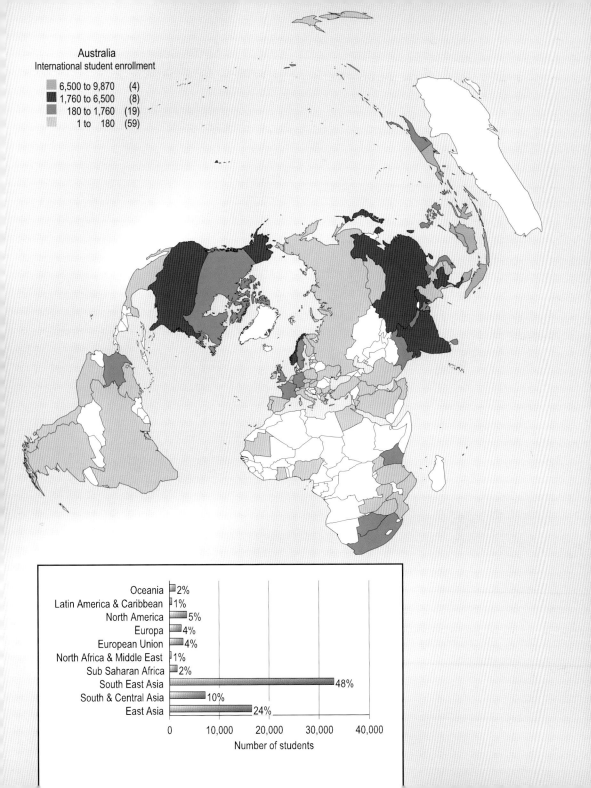

Australia
International student enrollment

6,500 to 9,870 (4)
1,760 to 6,500 (8)
180 to 1,760 (19)
1 to 180 (59)

Oceania 2%
Latin America & Caribbean 1%
North America 5%
Europa 4%
European Union 4%
North Africa & Middle East 1%
Sub Saharan Africa 2%
South East Asia 48%
South & Central Asia 10%
East Asia 24%

0   10,000   20,000   30,000   40,000
Number of students

Austria

Austria hosted 30,064 international students in 2000 of which 43% came from its two leading neighbors, Italy (7,064) and Germany (5,888). Beyond these two places Austrian enrollments are especially strong from Eastern and Southeastern Europe. Over 86% of all Austrian international enrollments come from European nations and 52% from other nations within the European Union. Beyond these European places only Iran with 768 students is found on the list of leading sources. Almost 60% of Austrian international students come from high-income nations.

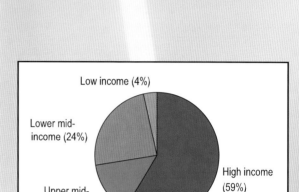

PROPORTION OF ENROLLED STUDENTS FROM WORLD BANK CLASSIFIED ECONOMIES

TEN LEADING PLACES OF ORIGIN	
Italy	7,064
Germany	5,888
Bulgaria	1,370
Turkey	1,172
Hungary	1,092
Serbia & Montenegro	949
Croatia	827
Poland	802
Iran	768
Bosnia & Herzegovina	732

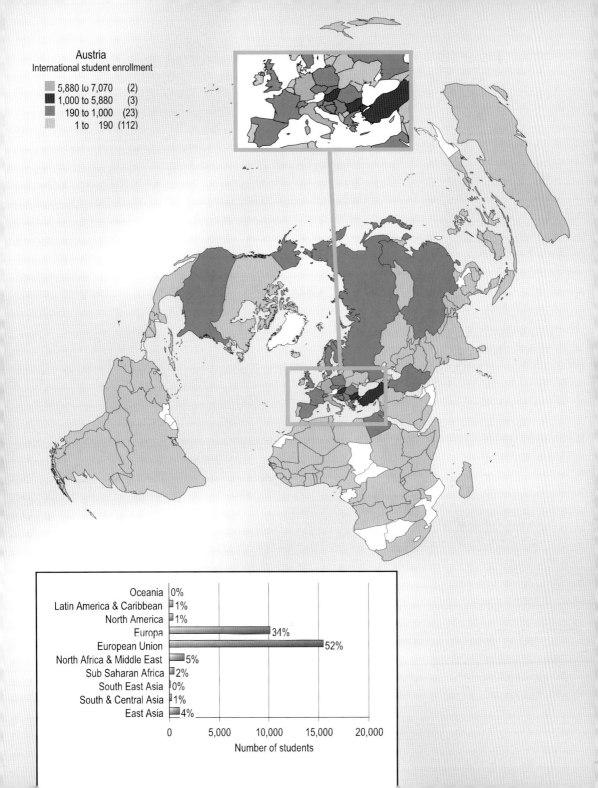

Austria
International student enrollment

- 5,880 to 7,070   (2)
- 1,000 to 5,880   (3)
- 190 to 1,000   (23)
- 1 to 190 (112)

Oceania	0%
Latin America & Caribbean	1%
North America	1%
Europa	34%
European Union	52%
North Africa & Middle East	5%
Sub Saharan Africa	2%
South East Asia	0%
South & Central Asia	1%
East Asia	4%

Number of students

Belgium

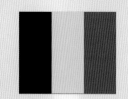

Remarkably, a small nation like Belgium hosts 37,789 international students. It is also of note that of these 26% are from France with which Belgium shares a common tongue. Beyond France and Italy, about 56% of Belgium's international students come from the European Union, especially the Netherlands, Luxembourg and Spain. Following Europe, Belgium enrolls 2,684 students from Congo, DPR, its former colony, and 5,355 students from Morocco, a former French colony.

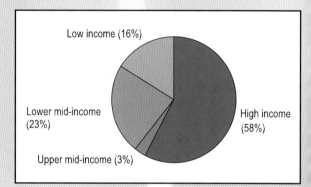

PROPORTION OF ENROLLED STUDENTS FROM WORLD BANK CLASSIFIED ECONOMIES

TEN LEADING PLACES OF ORIGIN	
France	9,837
Morocco	5,355
Italy	3,282
Netherlands	2,692
Congo, DPR	2,684
Luxembourg	1,468
Spain	1,433
Greece	717
Cameroon	705
China	643

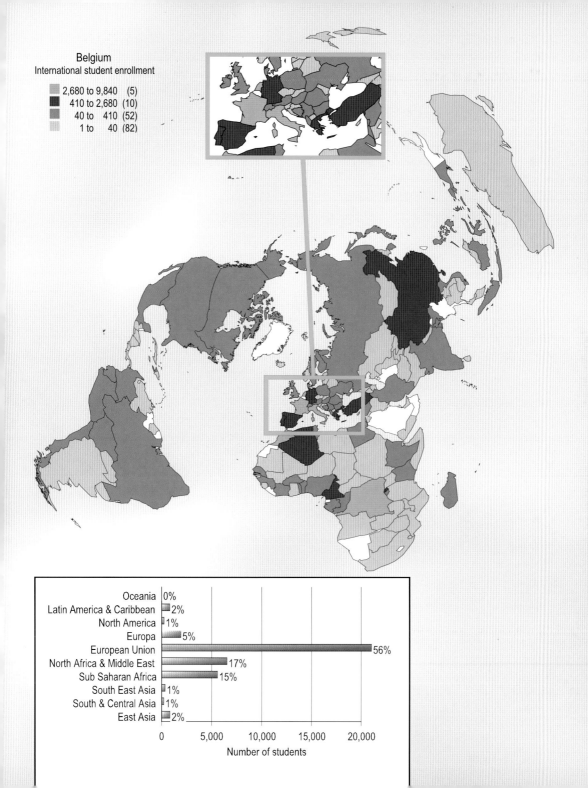

Belgium
International student enrollment

- 2,680 to 9,840 (5)
- 410 to 2,680 (10)
- 40 to 410 (52)
- 1 to 40 (82)

Oceania 0%
Latin America & Caribbean 2%
North America 1%
Europa 5%
European Union 56%
North Africa & Middle East 17%
Sub Saharan Africa 15%
South East Asia 1%
South & Central Asia 1%
East Asia 2%

0   5,000   10,000   15,000   20,000
Number of students

Canada

The 34,536 international students studying in Canada in 2000 were drawn from around the world. France (3,992) and the United States (3,822) are the largest sources of students going to Canada. Beyond these two, Canada is comparably attractive to students from the European Union and Europe broadly, and to students from East Asia. Twenty-two percent of Canada's students come from East Asia while 21% come from the European Union. Canada draws students from the Islamic world, especially Morocco, Saudi Arabia and Iran. Canada's enrollments appear to be well balanced by both region of origin, and following by the relative wealth of the sending countries.

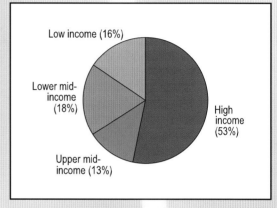

PROPORTION OF ENROLLED STUDENTS FROM WORLD BANK CLASSIFIED ECONOMIES

TEN LEADING PLACES OF ORIGIN	
France	3,992
United States	3,822
China	2,310
Hong Kong	2,176
Japan	1,414
United Kingdom	1,047
Malaysia	852
Morocco	827
Korea, Republic of	774
Germany	758

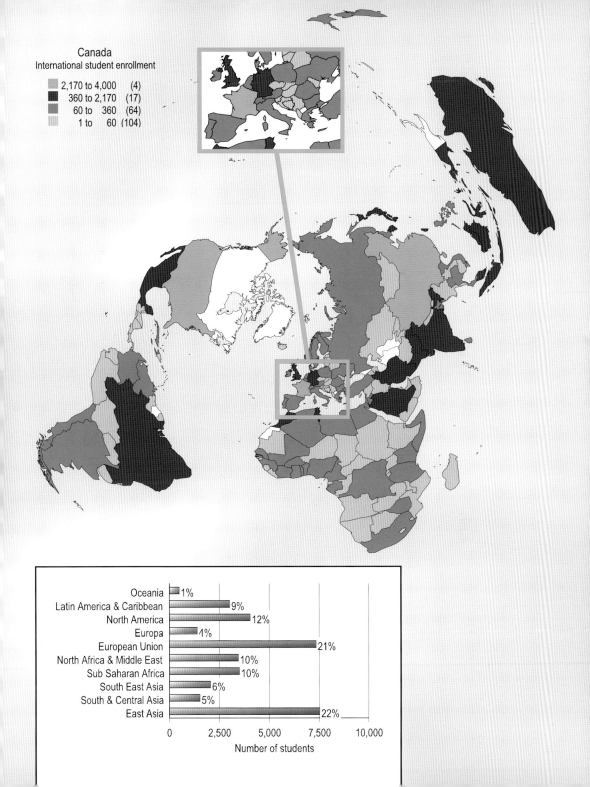

Canada
International student enrollment

2,170 to 4,000	(4)
360 to 2,170	(17)
60 to 360	(64)
1 to 60	(104)

Oceania 1%
Latin America & Caribbean 9%
North America 12%
Europa 1%
European Union 21%
North Africa & Middle East 10%
Sub Saharan Africa 10%
South East Asia 6%
South & Central Asia 5%
East Asia 22%

0   2,500   5,000   7,500   10,000
Number of students

Denmark

More than 79% of Denmark's 7,124 students come from the high-income nations of Europe. With that said, Denmark appears to be especially attractive to its immediate neighbors in northern Europe, particularly Norway, Iceland, Sweden and Germany. Beyond the European region Denmark enrolls 232 students from Iran and 202 from the United States. Denmark is the third smallest host country included in this survey and receives students from 121 places around the world. This represents a remarkably diverse set of international students.

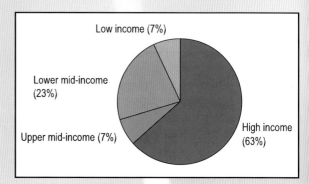

PROPORTION OF ENROLLED STUDENTS FROM WORLD BANK CLASSIFIED ECONOMIES

TEN LEADING PLACES OF ORIGIN	
Norway	1,293
Iceland	693
Sweden	593
Germany	558
Bosnia & Herzegovina	541
United Kingdom	374
Iran	232
Poland	211
United States	202
Turkey	184

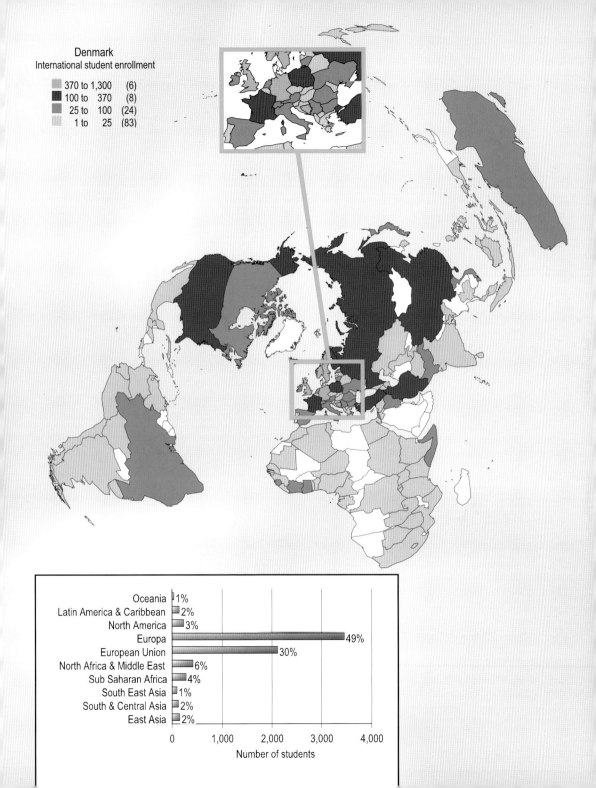

Denmark
International student enrollment

- 370 to 1,300 (6)
- 100 to 370 (8)
- 25 to 100 (24)
- 1 to 25 (83)

Oceania 1%
Latin America & Caribbean 2%
North America 3%
Europa 49%
European Union 30%
North Africa & Middle East 6%
Sub Saharan Africa 4%
South East Asia 1%
South & Central Asia 2%
East Asia 2%

0   1,000   2,000   3,000   4,000
Number of students

France

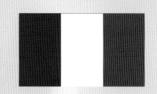

While France is the fourth largest host nation for international students, it enrolls a very small proportion of students from peer nations within the European Union. Of the member states, only Portugal hosts proportionally fewer European Union students than France. Of the 134,783 international students studying in France, 31% are from North Africa and the Middle East, while 24% are from Sub-Saharan Africa, places where French colonial ties remain strong. Because of the large number of students from less developed places, France has one of the smallest proportions of students from high-income economies of the host nations included in this survey.

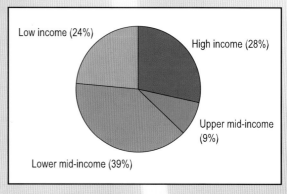

PROPORTION OF ENROLLED STUDENTS FROM WORLD BANK CLASSIFIED ECONOMIES

TEN LEADING PLACES OF ORIGIN	
Morocco	21,048
Algeria	13,539
Niger	6,268
Germany	5,436
Somalia	4,079
Italy	3,950
Spain	3,761
Cameroon	3,279
United Kingdom	3,147
Portugal	3,041

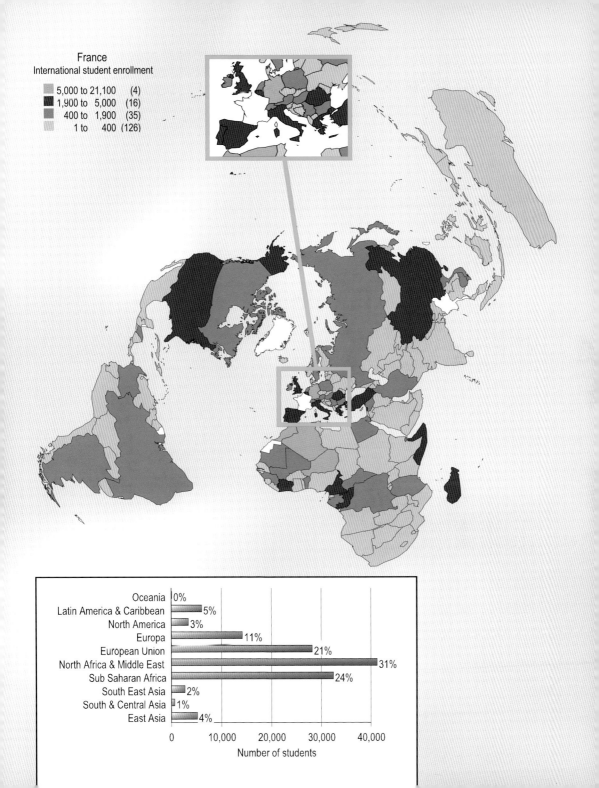

France
International student enrollment

- 5,000 to 21,100 (4)
- 1,900 to 5,000 (16)
- 400 to 1,900 (35)
- 1 to 400 (126)

Oceania 0%
Latin America & Caribbean 5%
North America 3%
Europa 11%
European Union 21%
North Africa & Middle East 31%
Sub Saharan Africa 24%
South East Asia 2%
South & Central Asia 1%
East Asia 4%

0   10,000   20,000   30,000   40,000
Number of students

Germany

International enrollments in Germany in 2001 amounted to 185,179 students. This number represents both permanent resident and visa students. About 64% of this total are foreign students from abroad. Germany is a major player in providing global higher education. Its main attraction, however, is to other European countries, especially Turkey and Poland that send 23,640 and 9,328 students respectively. European enrollments account for almost 65% of Germany's international students with 23% of them coming from within the European Union. Beyond Europe, Germany hosts 9,109 Chinese students and significant numbers of students from the Islamic world, with more than 6,000 each from Iran and Morocco. About one-third of Germany's international students come from high-income countries.

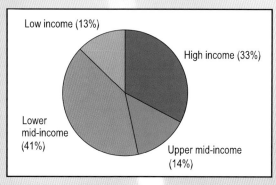

PROPORTION OF ENROLLED STUDENTS FROM WORLD BANK CLASSIFIED ECONOMIES

TEN LEADING PLACES OF ORIGIN	
Turkey	23,640
Poland	9,328
China	9,109
Greece	7,516
Russia	6,987
Italy	6,771
Iran	6,359
France	6,246
Morocco	6,204
Austria	6,127

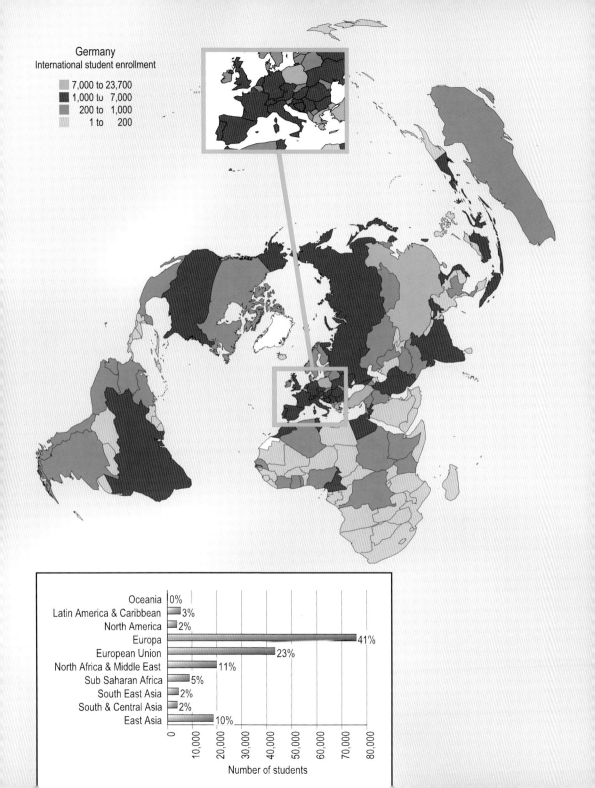

Germany
International student enrollment

- 7,000 to 23,700
- 1,000 to 7,000
- 200 to 1,000
- 1 to 200

Oceania 0%
Latin America & Caribbean 3%
North America 2%
Europa 41%
European Union 23%
North Africa & Middle East 11%
Sub Saharan Africa 5%
South East Asia 2%
South & Central Asia 2%
East Asia 10%

0   10,000   20,000   30,000   40,000   50,000   60,000   70,000   80,000

Number of students

Ireland

Of the English-speaking host countries, Ireland is the smallest host and enrolls only 5,564 international students. Students from the United States, the United Kingdom, and Canada account for 48% of all internationals in Ireland. Of note however are the relatively large numbers of Malaysian students studying in Ireland. Ireland also attracts students from within the European Union, notably, Germany, France, and Spain. Ireland hosts students that largely come from wealthy nations. Fully three-quarters of Ireland's international students come from high-income countries.

PROPORTION OF ENROLLED STUDENTS FROM WORLD BANK CLASSIFIED ECONOMIES

TEN LEADING PLACES OF ORIGIN	
United States	1,779
United Kingdom	732
Malaysia	608
Germany	240
Canada	173
France	171
Kuwait	156
Norway	143
Spain	103
Italy	94

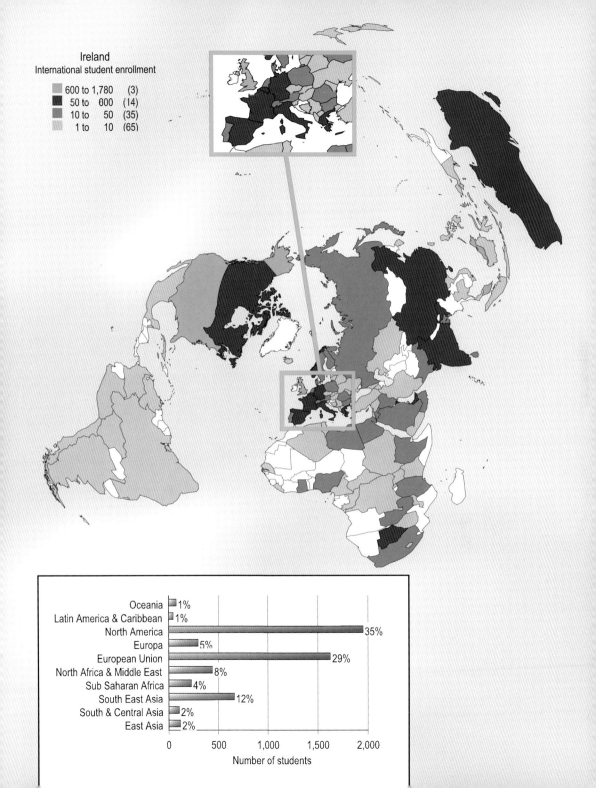

Ireland
International student enrollment

600 to 1,780 (3)
50 to 600 (14)
10 to 50 (35)
1 to 10 (65)

Oceania 1%
Latin America & Caribbean 1%
North America 35%
Europa 5%
European Union 29%
North Africa & Middle East 8%
Sub Saharan Africa 4%
South East Asia 12%
South & Central Asia 2%
East Asia 2%

0   500   1,000   1,500   2,000
Number of students

Italy

Italy enrolls 21,299 international students. Most notable in Italy's profile is the large number of students from southeastern Europe studying in Italy. In all, the leading three source countries for Italy — Greece, Albania and Croatia — contribute 53% of all Italian international enrollments. Seventy-seven percent of all internationals studying in Italy come from Europe, and 46% of these come from other European Union nations. Almost 10% of Italian international students come from the Middle East, particularly Israel, Iran, Lebanon and Morocco.

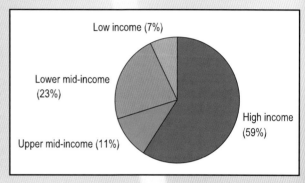

PROPORTION OF ENROLLED STUDENTS FROM WORLD BANK CLASSIFIED ECONOMIES

TEN LEADING PLACES OF ORIGIN	
Greece	8,126
Albania	2,127
Croatia	1,011
Switzerland	743
Cameroon	665
Germany	663
San Marino	637
Israel	626
Iran	420
France	360

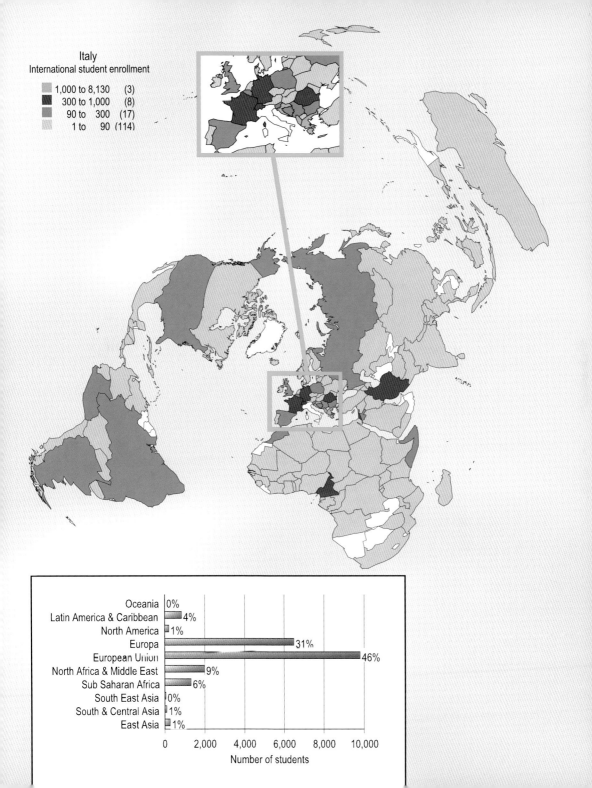

Italy
International student enrollment

- 1,000 to 8,130 (3)
- 300 to 1,000 (8)
- 90 to 300 (17)
- 1 to 90 (114)

Oceania 0%
Latin America & Caribbean 4%
North America 1%
Europa 31%
European Union 46%
North Africa & Middle East 9%
Sub Saharan Africa 6%
South East Asia 0%
South & Central Asia 1%
East Asia 1%

0   2,000   4,000   6,000   8,000   10,000
Number of students

Japan

Japan is a mid-sized host nation that is a regional player. In 2000, 59,656 international students were enrolled in Japan. Of the global hosts, Japan's enrollment profile reflects the highest degree of concentration of any host nation. More than 50% of its enrollments come from China and Korea, and 78% come from East Asia. This is reflected in the income standing of the source nations. Japan hosts one of the largest concentrations of students from the lower mid-income bracket, and reflects the World Bank's classification of China as a lower middle-income economy.

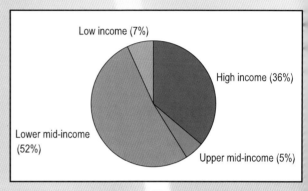

PROPORTION OF ENROLLED STUDENTS FROM WORLD BANK CLASSIFIED ECONOMIES

TEN LEADING PLACES OF ORIGIN	
China	28,076
Korea, Republic of	18,237
Malaysia	1,956
Indonesia	1,143
United States	1,077
Thailand	1,019
Bangladesh	760
Vietnam	531
Philippines	430
Brazil	371

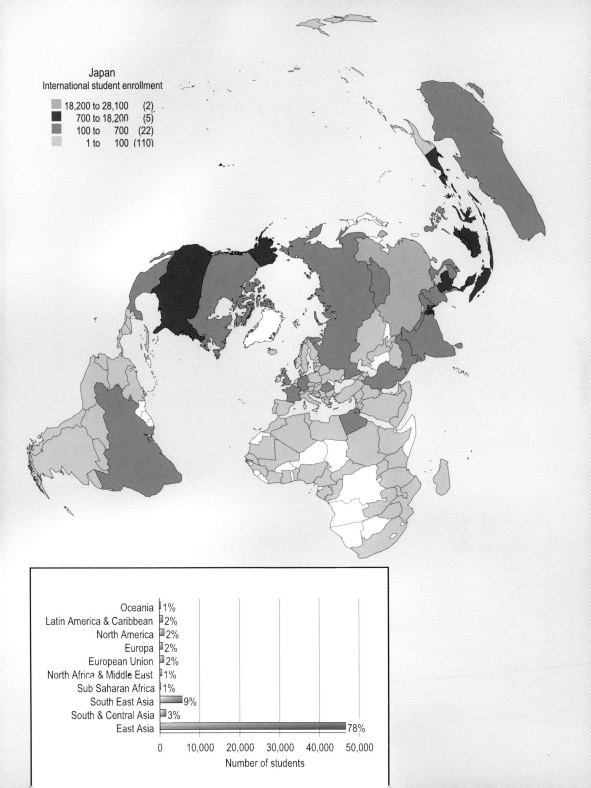

Japan
International student enrollment

■ 18,200 to 28,100 (2)
■ 700 to 18,200 (5)
■ 100 to 700 (22)
■ 1 to 100 (110)

Oceania ▮1%
Latin America & Caribbean ▮2%
North America ▮2%
Europa ▮2%
European Union ▮2%
North Africa & Middle East ▮1%
Sub Saharan Africa ▮1%
South East Asia ▮▮▮9%
South & Central Asia ▮3%
East Asia ▮▮▮▮▮▮▮▮▮▮▮▮78%

0   10,000   20,000   30,000   40,000   50,000
Number of students

Jordan

Jordan draws more students proportionally from North Africa and the Middle East than any other country in this survey. In fact, 82% of Jordan's international students come from this region with the Palestinian Authority providing the largest number of students. It is not clear if Jordan's Palestinian enrollments represent permanent residents or visa students. Malaysia, with 1,232 students, is the only non-Middle Eastern country represented on Jordan's list of 10 leading sources. Malaysia has a large Muslim population. For a country whose first university was founded in 1962, Jordan's mix of public and private institutions enrolls a surprising number of students from abroad.

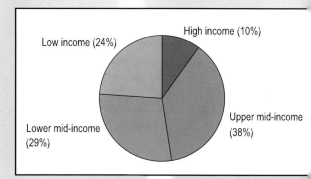

PROPORTION OF ENROLLED STUDENTS FROM WORLD BANK CLASSIFIED ECONOMIES

TEN LEADING PLACES OF ORIGIN	
Palestinian Authority	4,069
Yemen	1,481
Malaysia	1,232
Syria	1,160
Saudi Arabia	775
Oman	742
Iraq	598
Israel	372
Sudan	222
Lebanon	178

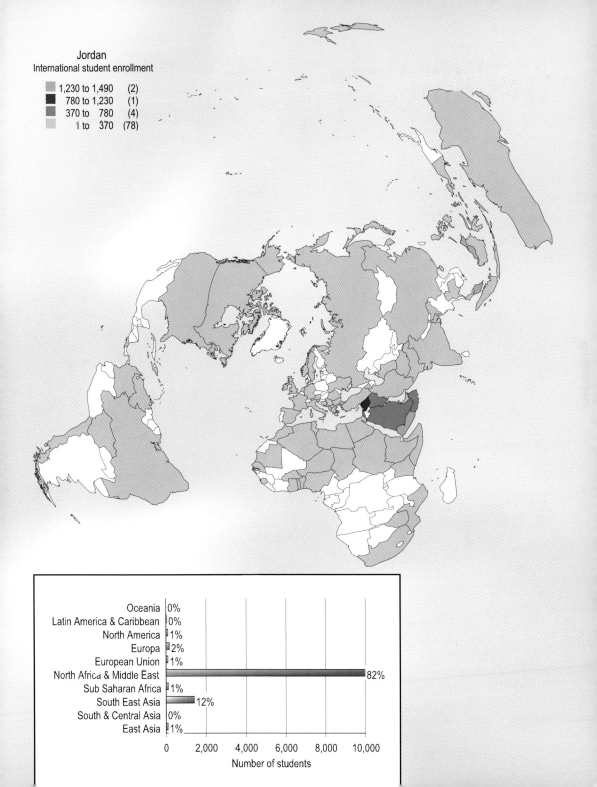

Jordan
International student enrollment

1,230 to 1,490 (2)
780 to 1,230 (1)
370 to 780 (4)
1 to 370 (78)

Oceania 0%
Latin America & Caribbean 0%
North America 1%
Europa 2%
European Union 1%
North Africa & Middle East 82%
Sub Saharan Africa 1%
South East Asia 12%
South & Central Asia 0%
East Asia 1%

0   2,000   4,000   6,000   8,000   10,000

Number of students

Netherlands

The relatively large number of international students (13,949) enrolled in the Netherlands come from around the world. Europe is the source of 60% of the Netherlands students, and 43% come from within the European Union. Germany, with its linguistic and cultural affinities, is the largest origin country for international students. North Africa and the Middle East is the source of 19% of Netherland's international enrollments. The Netherlands is a destination of choice for students from the Islamic world, notably Morocco (1,874), Turkey (1,158), and also Indonesia, Iran and Iraq. Students from the former colonial possessions of Suriname are also enrolled in large numbers.

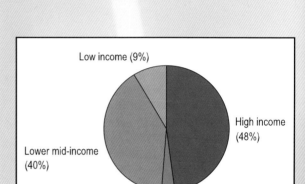

PROPORTION OF ENROLLED STUDENTS FROM WORLD BANK CLASSIFIED ECONOMIES

TEN LEADING PLACES OF ORIGIN	
Germany	2,292
Morocco	1,874
Belgium	1,373
Turkey	1,158
Suriname	846
United Kingdom	661
Spain	498
Indonesia	407
Iran	391
Italy	340

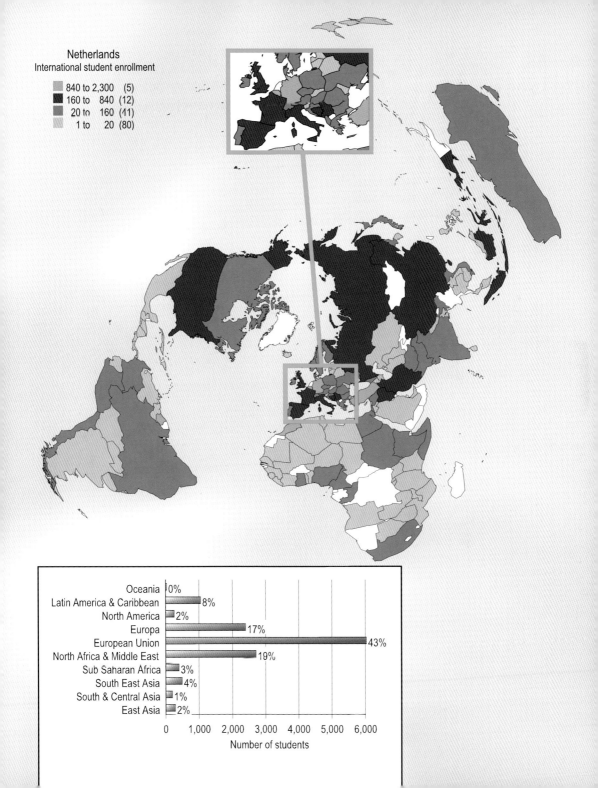

Netherlands
International student enrollment

- 840 to 2,300 (5)
- 160 to 840 (12)
- 20 to 160 (11)
- 1 to 20 (80)

Oceania 0%
Latin America & Caribbean 8%
North America 2%
Europa 17%
European Union 43%
North Africa & Middle East 19%
Sub Saharan Africa 3%
South East Asia 4%
South & Central Asia 1%
East Asia 2%

0   1,000   2,000   3,000   4,000   5,000   6,000
Number of students

New Zealand

Like Australia across the Tasman Sea, New Zealand's efforts in attracting international students have produced a highly concentrated distribution by world region. Of the 7,603 internationals studying in New Zealand, more than 50% come from East or Southeast Asia, and 14% come from the Pacific Islands and elsewhere in Oceania. The United States is an exception, and it alone is the non-Asian nation that makes the leading ten-nation list for New Zealand. Over the past four years, New Zealand began active engagement with international education, and has in recent years experienced rapid growth in international enrollments.

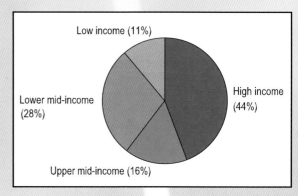

PROPORTION OF ENROLLED STUDENTS FROM WORLD BANK CLASSIFIED ECONOMIES

TEN LEADING PLACES OF ORIGIN	
Malaysia	1,097
China	842
United States	694
Japan	461
Korea, Republic of	419
Indonesia	344
Hong Kong	341
Taiwan	337
Thailand	311
Fiji	289

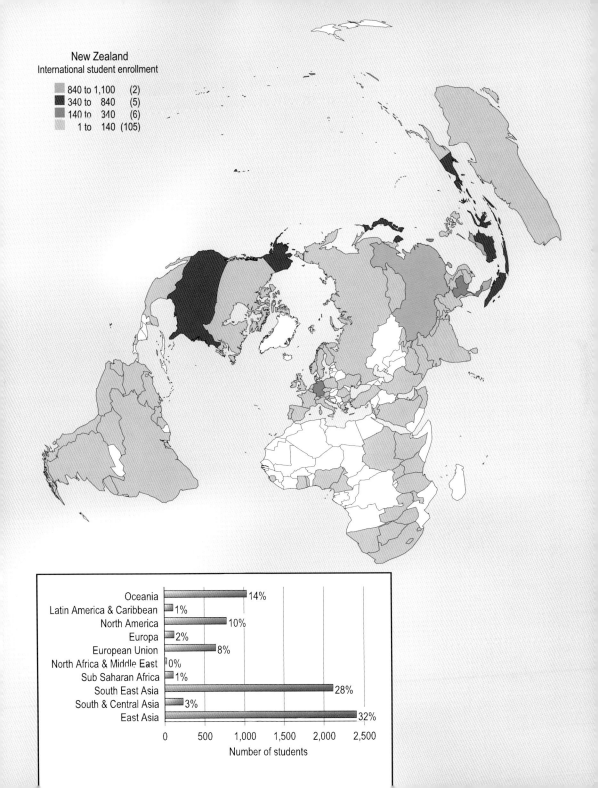

New Zealand
International student enrollment

- 840 to 1,100 (2)
- 340 to 840 (5)
- 140 to 340 (6)
- 1 to 140 (105)

Region	Percentage
Oceania	14%
Latin America & Caribbean	1%
North America	10%
Europa	2%
European Union	8%
North Africa & Middle East	0%
Sub Saharan Africa	1%
South East Asia	28%
South & Central Asia	3%
East Asia	32%

Number of students

Portugal

Almost two-thirds of Portugal's 10,998 international students come from countries that were former colonial possessions, and which share a linguistic affinity with Portugal. Among these are the three leading source places, Angola (2,393), Cape Verde Islands (1,728) and Brazil (1,338). Because of these connections, Portugal receives an unusually large proportion of its students (39%) from low-income countries. The second most significant source of students for Portugal are those from fellow European Union countries, especially France, Spain and Germany. Only 20% of Portugal's international students come from European Union nations, among the lowest proportion when compared with other countries within the European Union.

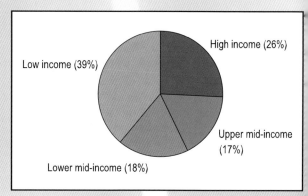

PROPORTION OF ENROLLED STUDENTS FROM WORLD BANK CLASSIFIED ECONOMIES

TEN LEADING PLACES OF ORIGIN	
Angola	2,393
Cape Verde	1,728
Brazil	1,338
France	984
Mozambique	834
Venezuela	467
Guinea-Bissau	422
Spain	390
Germany	358
São Tomé & Príncipe	358

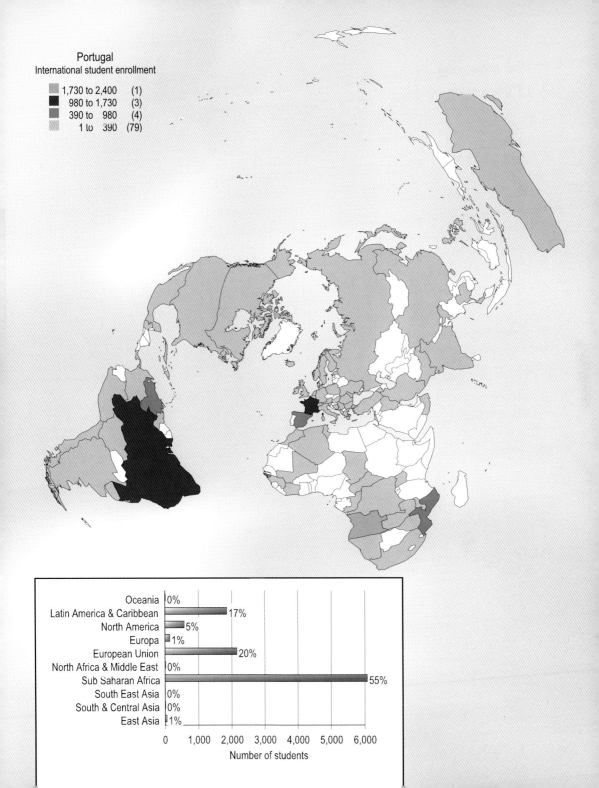

Portugal
International student enrollment

1,730 to 2,400	(1)
980 to 1,730	(3)
390 to 980	(4)
1 to 390	(79)

Oceania 0%
Latin America & Caribbean 17%
North America 5%
Europa 1%
European Union 20%
North Africa & Middle East 0%
Sub Saharan Africa 55%
South East Asia 0%
South & Central Asia 0%
East Asia 1%

0   1,000   2,000   3,000   4,000   5,000   6,000

Number of students

Republic of Korea

Korea is the smallest host nation in this survey of international mobility in terms of student enrollments. The 2,737 students enrolled in Korean institutions come primarily from China (1,182) and Japan (613). Indeed these two nations contribute 65% of all international students studying in Korea. The United States is the third largest source of students for Korea with 195. Korea draws smaller numbers of students from elsewhere in Asia. In all, about 80% of Korea's international students come from Asia.

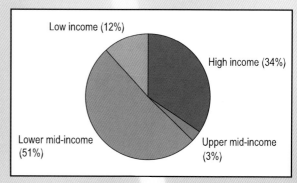

Low income (12%)
High income (34%)
Lower mid-income (51%)
Upper mid-income (3%)

PROPORTION OF ENROLLED STUDENTS FROM WORLD BANK CLASSIFIED ECONOMIES

TEN LEADING PLACES OF ORIGIN	
China	1,182
Japan	613
United States	195
Russia	77
Vietnam	62
Mongolia	56
Canada	39
Uzbekistan	35
India	34
Indonesia	32

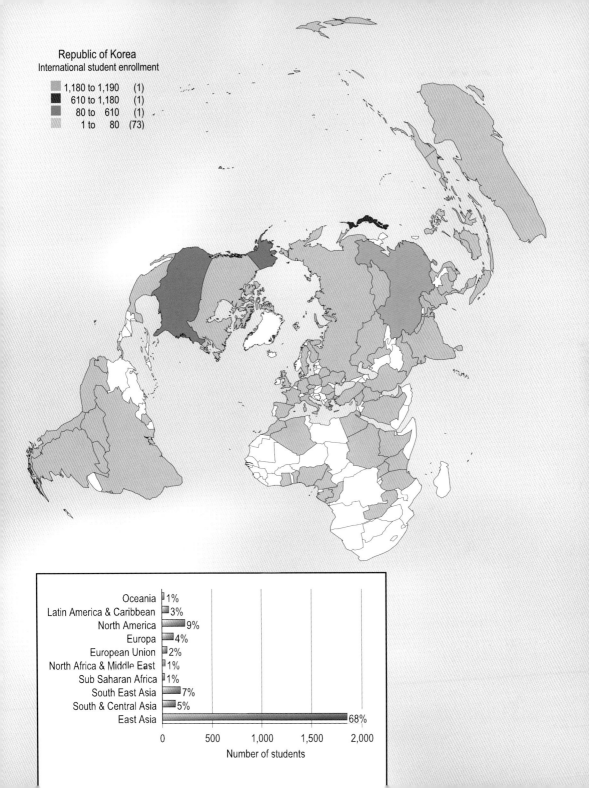

Republic of Korea
International student enrollment

	1,180 to 1,190	(1)
	610 to 1,180	(1)
	80 to 610	(1)
	1 to 80	(73)

Oceania 1%
Latin America & Caribbean 3%
North America 9%
Europa 4%
European Union 2%
North Africa & Middle East 1%
Sub Saharan Africa 1%
South East Asia 7%
South & Central Asia 5%
East Asia 68%

0 500 1,000 1,500 2,000
Number of students

Spain

Spain hosts 40,506 international students. These students are drawn primarily from within the European Union, or from Latin America and the Caribbean. Spain hosts 21,200 students from the European Union or 52% of its total. Spain is proportionally the largest host of students from Latin America with 10,127 students (25%) from these nations. The leading senders from Latin America are Argentina, Mexico, Colombia and Brazil. Beyond these regions, Spain hosts 3,144 students from Morocco. Almost 60% of Spain's international students come from high-income nations.

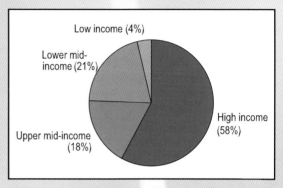

PROPORTION OF ENROLLED STUDENTS FROM WORLD BANK CLASSIFIED ECONOMIES

TEN LEADING PLACES OF ORIGIN	
France	4,582
Italy	4,572
Germany	3,879
Morocco	3,144
United Kingdom	2,660
Argentina	1,537
Mexico	1,445
Belgium	1,250
Colombia	1,156
Brazil	1,102

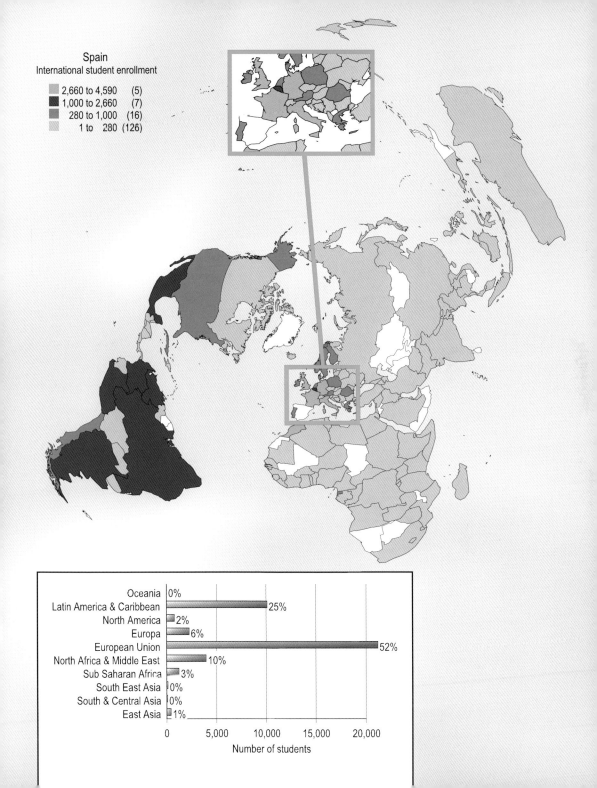

Spain
International student enrollment

- 2,660 to 4,590 (5)
- 1,000 to 2,660 (7)
- 280 to 1,000 (16)
- 1 to 280 (126)

Region	Percentage
Oceania	0%
Latin America & Caribbean	25%
North America	2%
Europa	6%
European Union	52%
North Africa & Middle East	10%
Sub Saharan Africa	3%
South East Asia	0%
South & Central Asia	0%
East Asia	1%

Number of students

Sweden

Sweden hosted 20,631 international students in 2000, of which almost 30% came from its three leading sources: Finland, Germany and Norway. Beyond these northern European countries, Sweden draws 51% of its students from within the European Union and 76% from throughout Europe. Beyond the borders of Europe, Sweden hosts 895 students from the United States and 630 from China. As is typical of many European hosts that enroll a large proportion of their international students from within the European Union, more than two-thirds of Sweden's international students come from among the wealthiest nations of the world.

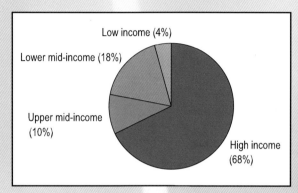

PROPORTION OF ENROLLED STUDENTS FROM WORLD BANK CLASSIFIED ECONOMIES

TEN LEADING PLACES OF ORIGIN	
Finland	3,368
Germany	1,888
Norway	1,214
France	922
United States	895
Denmark	860
United Kingdom	828
Poland	668
Bosnia & Herzegovina	665
China	630

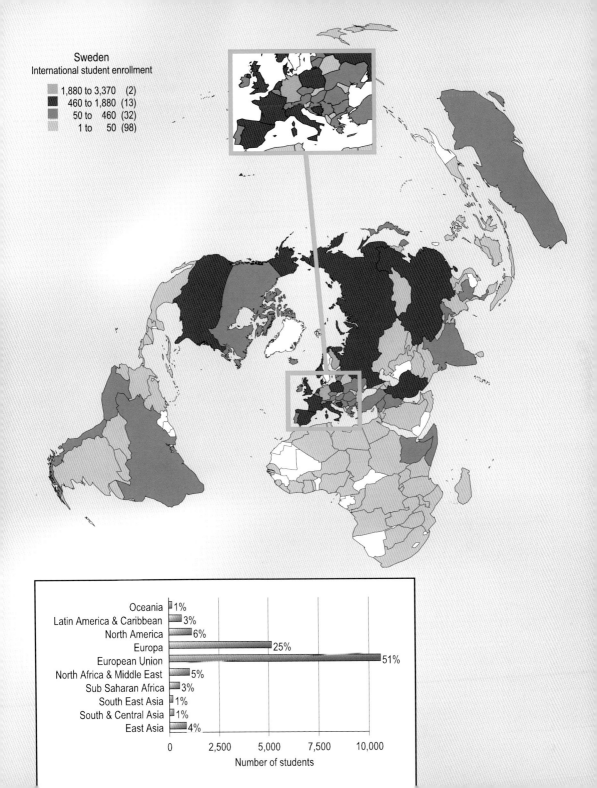

Sweden
International student enrollment

1,880 to 3,370 (2)
460 to 1,880 (13)
50 to 460 (32)
1 to 50 (98)

Oceania 1%
Latin America & Caribbean 3%
North America 6%
Europa 25%
European Union 51%
North Africa & Middle East 5%
Sub Saharan Africa 3%
South East Asia 1%
South & Central Asia 1%
East Asia 4%

0   2,500   5,000   7,500   10,000
Number of students

Switzerland

Among the wealthiest nations, Switzerland enrolls fewer students proportionally from poorer nations than other developed countries. Of Switzerland's 24,729 international students in 2000, 68% come from the European Union and 82% come from Europe. Consequently, 73% of Swiss international students come from high-income economies, especially Germany (5,512), Italy (4,017) and France (2,816).

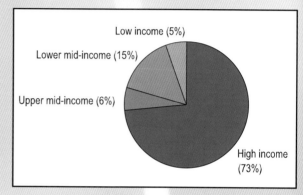

PROPORTION OF ENROLLED STUDENTS FROM WORLD BANK CLASSIFIED ECONOMIES

TEN LEADING PLACES OF ORIGIN	
Germany	5,512
Italy	4,017
France	2,816
Spain	1,508
Austria	728
Turkey	522
China	426
Portugal	421
Liechtenstein	416
United States	348

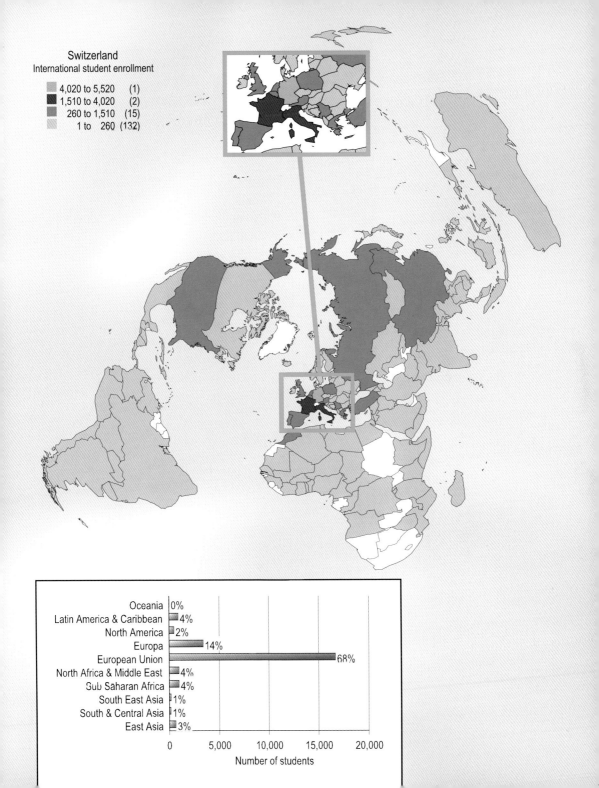

Switzerland
International student enrollment

- 4,020 to 5,520 (1)
- 1,510 to 4,020 (2)
- 260 to 1,510 (15)
- 1 to 260 (132)

Oceania 0%
Latin America & Caribbean 4%
North America 2%
Europa 14%
European Union 68%
North Africa & Middle East 4%
Sub Saharan Africa 4%
South East Asia 1%
South & Central Asia 1%
East Asia 3%

0   5,000   10,000   15,000   20,000
Number of students

Turkey

Turkey enrolled 17,635 international students in 2000, making it a mid-sized host nation. The pattern of enrollments reflects the disposition of students with Turkic affiliations to seek an education in Turkey. Turkey is one of the largest providers of international tertiary education to students from selected countries in the Caucasus and Central Asia. Cyprus is the largest place of origin for students studying in Turkey. Reflecting the enrollment standing of students from the Caucasus and Central Asia, Turkey enrolls one of the largest percentages of students from relatively poor economies.

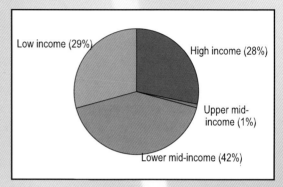

PROPORTION OF ENROLLED STUDENTS FROM WORLD BANK CLASSIFIED ECONOMIES

TEN LEADING PLACES OF ORIGIN	
Cyprus	3,053
Azerbaijan	1,871
Turkmenistan	1,673
Greece	1,319
Kazakhstan	1,142
Russia	1,004
Kyrgyzstan	892
Bulgaria	615
Albania	558
Bosnia & Herzegovina	533

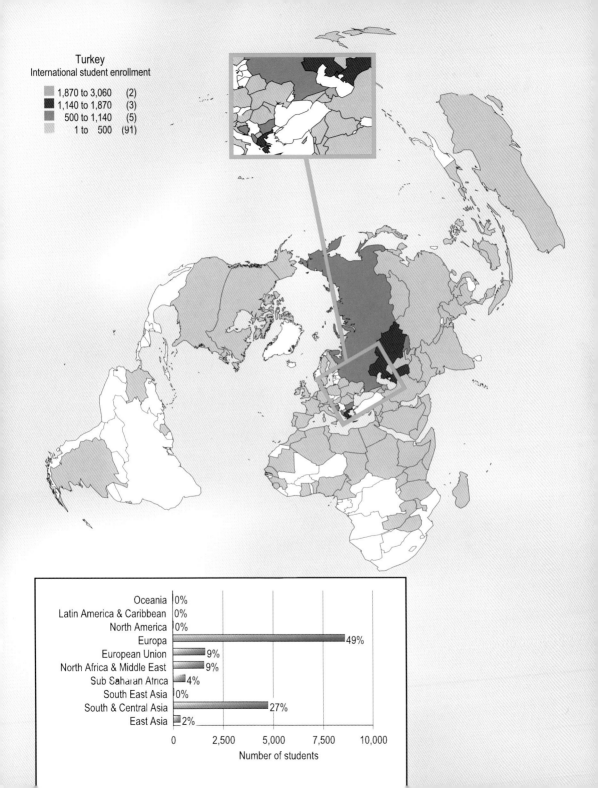

Turkey
International student enrollment

■ 1,870 to 3,060   (2)
■ 1,140 to 1,870   (3)
■ 500 to 1,140   (5)
▨ 1 to 500   (91)

Oceania 0%
Latin America & Caribbean 0%
North America 0%
Europa 49%
European Union 9%
North Africa & Middle East 9%
Sub Saharan Africa 4%
South East Asia 0%
South & Central Asia 27%
East Asia 2%

0   2,500   5,000   7,500   10,000
Number of students

United Kingdom

The United Kingdom hosted 222,576 international students in 2000, the second largest host nation following the United States. While considerable attention has been paid to the United Kingdom's attraction as a destination for Asian students, it is among European students that the real strength of the United Kingdom as a destination lies. About 43% of all internationals in the United Kingdom come from within the European Union. The United Kingdom also hosts students from predominately wealthy countries, with almost 70% of its enrollments from high-income places. Unlike many European hosts with extensive colonial pasts, the United Kingdom has grown well beyond its former possessions and is a destination of choice for students around the world.

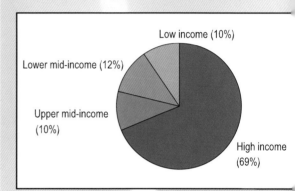

PROPORTION OF ENROLLED STUDENTS FROM WORLD BANK CLASSIFIED ECONOMIES

TEN LEADING PLACES OF ORIGIN	
Greece	28,250
Germany	13,244
France	12,388
Ireland	12,184
United States	11,553
China	10,332
Malaysia	9,168
Hong Kong	8,278
Spain	7,198
Japan	6,154

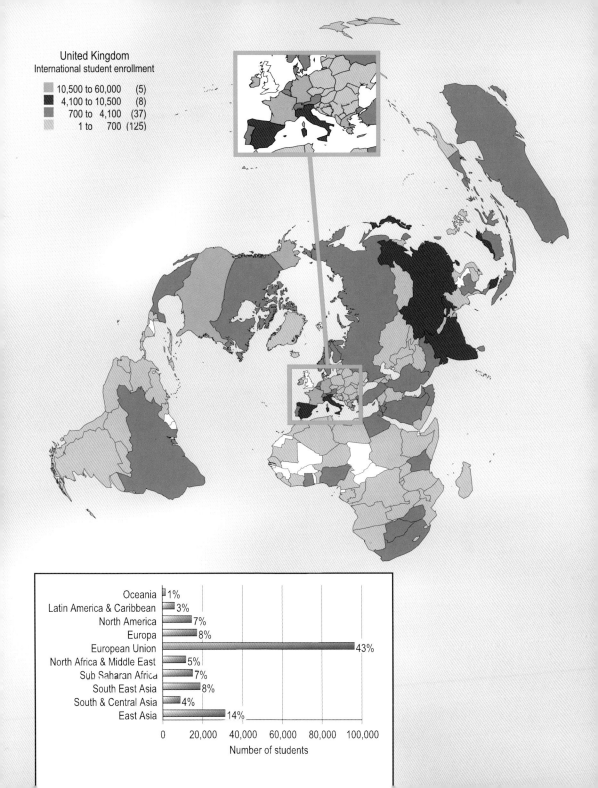

United Kingdom
International student enrollment

10,500 to 60,000 (5)
4,100 to 10,500 (8)
700 to 4,100 (37)
1 to 700 (125)

Oceania 1%
Latin America & Caribbean 3%
North America 7%
Europa 8%
European Union 43%
North Africa & Middle East 5%
Sub Saharan Africa 7%
South East Asia 8%
South & Central Asia 4%
East Asia 14%

0   20,000   40,000   60,000   80,000   100,000
Number of students

United States

More internationally mobile students study in the United States than in any other host country. In all, 547,092 international students studied in the States in 2000. Because of these large numbers, it is often easy to overlook the fact that these enrollments are actually highly concentrated. Just four nations (China, India, Japan and Korea) are the source of nearly half of all US enrollments. Collectively, the ten leading sources contribute almost 66% of enrollments. With this noted, it is also true that the United States hosts significant numbers of students from Latin America and the Caribbean (12%), while only 9% of its enrollments come from European Union nations.

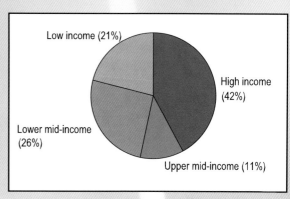

PROPORTION OF ENROLLED STUDENTS FROM WORLD BANK CLASSIFIED ECONOMIES

TEN LEADING PLACES OF ORIGIN	
China	59,939
India	54,664
Japan	46,497
Korea, Republic of	45,685
Taiwan	28,566
Canada	25,279
Indonesia	11,625
Thailand	11,187
Turkey	10,983
Mexico	10,670

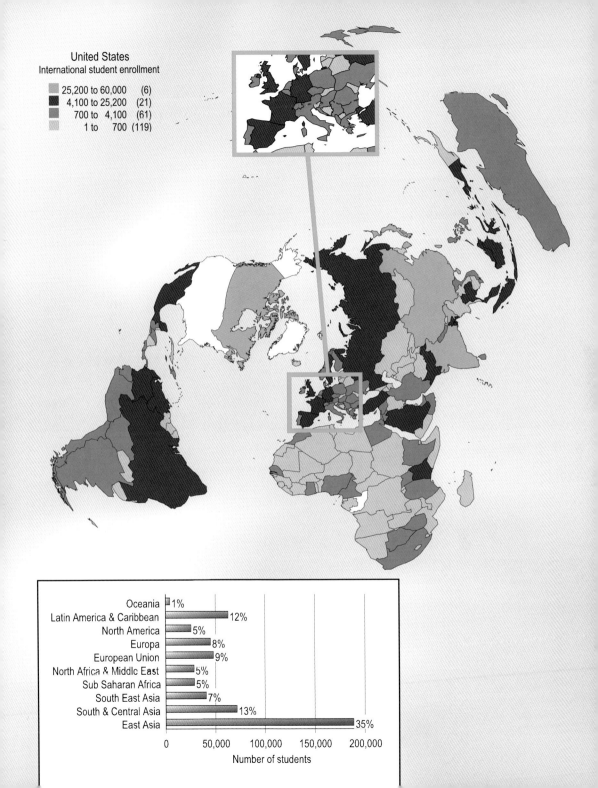

United States
International student enrollment

25,200 to 60,000	(6)
4,100 to 25,200	(21)
700 to 4,100	(61)
1 to 700	(119)

Oceania 1%
Latin America & Caribbean 12%
North America 5%
Europa 8%
European Union 9%
North Africa & Middle East 5%
Sub Saharan Africa 5%
South East Asia 7%
South & Central Asia 13%
East Asia 35%

0   50,000   100,000   150,000   200,000

Number of students

ORIGIN

China and India will account for more than half of the total global demand for international higher education by 2025.

Source: Global Student Mobility 2025
IDP Education Australia

Reflection: In 2000 the leading 10 places of origin accounted for 40% of all internationally mobile students. Is international education truly a global phenomenon?

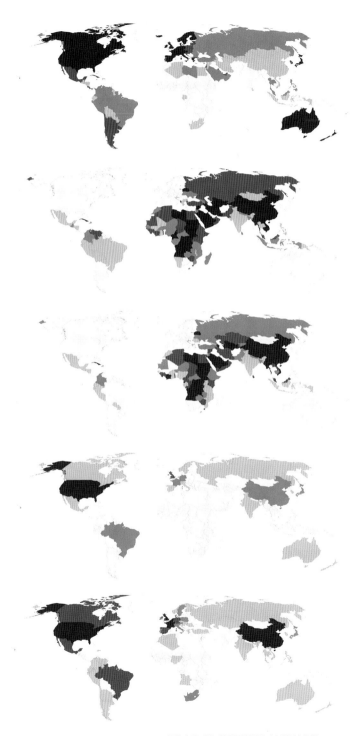

Human Development Index

- 0.883 to 0.942 (26)
- 0.795 to 0.883 (29)
- 0.742 to 0.795 (31)
- 0.622 to 0.742 (35)
- 0.275 to 0.622 (51)

Civil Liberties

- Least Free (25)
- (34)
- (26)
- (27)
- Most Free (59)

Press Freedom

- Least Free (20)
- (23)
- (23)
- (32)
- Most Free (72)

Aircraft Departures

- 8,534,500 to 8,534,500 (1)
- 985,300 to 8,534,500 (1)
- 641,300 to 985,300 (5)
- 214,300 to 641,300 (13)
- 100 to 214,300 (135)

Foreign Investment

- Highest Net Inflows (6)
- (6)
- (11)
- (30)
- Smallest Net Inflows (101)

THE ATLAS OF STUDENT MOBILITY

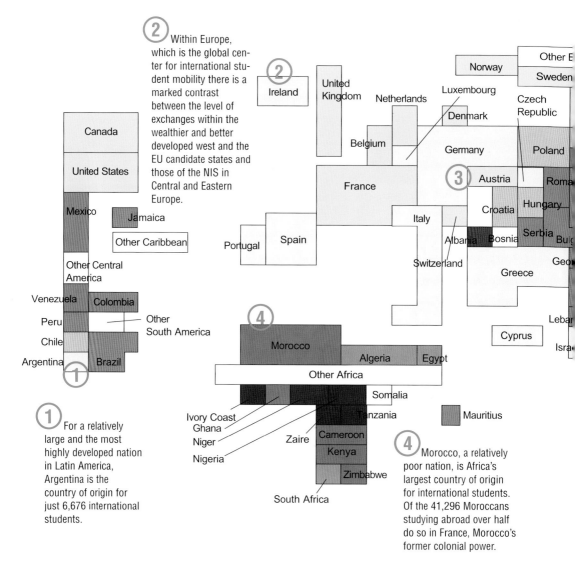

② Within Europe, which is the global center for international student mobility there is a marked contrast between the level of exchanges within the wealthier and better developed west and the EU candidate states and those of the NIS in Central and Eastern Europe.

① For a relatively large and the most highly developed nation in Latin America, Argentina is the country of origin for just 6,676 international students.

④ Morocco, a relatively poor nation, is Africa's largest country of origin for international students. Of the 41,296 Moroccans studying abroad over half do so in France, Morocco's former colonial power.

Canada
United States
Mexico
Jamaica
Other Caribbean
Other Central America
Venezuela
Colombia
Peru
Other South America
Chile
Argentina
Brazil

Ireland
United Kingdom
Netherlands
Luxembourg
Norway
Other E
Sweden
Czech Republic
Belgium
Denmark
Germany
Poland
France
Austria
Roma
Italy
Croatia
Hungary
Portugal
Spain
Albania
Bosnia
Serbia
Bu
Switzerland
Greece
Geo
Cyprus
Leba
Isra

Morocco
Algeria
Egypt
Other Africa
Somalia
Ivory Coast
Ghana
Tanzania
Mauritius
Niger
Zaire
Cameroon
Kenya
Nigeria
Zimbabwe
South Africa

ENVISION THE GLOBE THRU THE LENS OF THE TOTAL NUMBER OF STUDENTS ABROAD — AND YOU GET A NEW WORLD

From a global perspective, international educational mobility is largely the creation of the wealthier and better-developed countries with students moving between relatively similar places in terms of their economic and human development, with the notable exceptions of China and India and a few other emerging nations that also send large numbers of students to the developed world. This enterprise has largely bypassed South and Central America, Sub-Saharan Africa and much of the Islamic world.

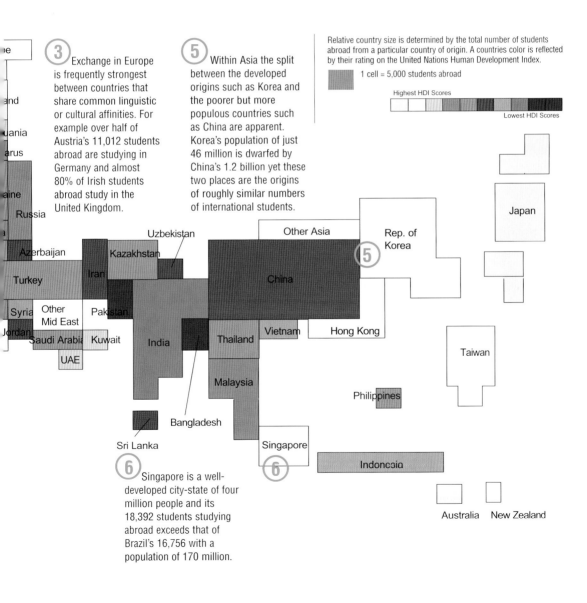

(3) Exchange in Europe is frequently strongest between countries that share common linguistic or cultural affinities. For example over half of Austria's 11,012 students abroad are studying in Germany and almost 80% of Irish students abroad study in the United Kingdom.

(5) Within Asia the split between the developed origins such as Korea and the poorer but more populous countries such as China are apparent. Korea's population of just 46 million is dwarfed by China's 1.2 billion yet these two places are the origins of roughly similar numbers of international students.

Relative country size is determined by the total number of students abroad from a particular country of origin. A countries color is reflected by their rating on the United Nations Human Development Index.

1 cell = 5,000 students abroad

Highest HDI Scores
Lowest HDI Scores

(6) Singapore is a well-developed city-state of four million people and its 18,392 students studying abroad exceeds that of Brazil's 16,756 with a population of 170 million.

Russia · Uzbekistan · Other Asia · Rep. of Korea · Japan · Azerbaijan · Kazakhstan · Turkey · Iran · China · Syria · Other Mid East · Pakistan · Vietnam · Hong Kong · Jordan · Saudi Arabia · Kuwait · India · Thailand · Taiwan · UAE · Malaysia · Philippines · Bangladesh · Sri Lanka · Singapore · Indonesia · Australia · New Zealand

Percent Urban

- 86.8 to 100 (21)
- 72.9 to 86.7 (24)
- 60.1 to 72.9 (28)
- 44.1 to 60.1 (35)
- 6.2 to 44.1 (63)

Life Expectancy (years)

- 76.2 to 81 (30)
- 72.6 to 76.2 (29)
- 69.1 to 72.6 (32)
- 59.4 to 69.1 (34)
- 38.9 to 59.4 (46)

Phone Lines Per 1000 People

- 611 to 750 (10)
- 498 to 611 (12)
- 365 to 498 (15)
- 218 to 365 (24)
- 1 to 218 (109)

Population (mil)

- 1,000 to 1,280 (2)
- 110 to 1,000 (8)
- 40 to 110 (18)
- 10 to 40 (46)
- 0 to 10 (97)

Students Abroad

- 62,000 to 121,000 (3)
- 37,000 to 62,000 (8)
- 18,000 to 37,000 (11)
- 8,000 to 18,000 (25)
- 1 to 8,000 (166)

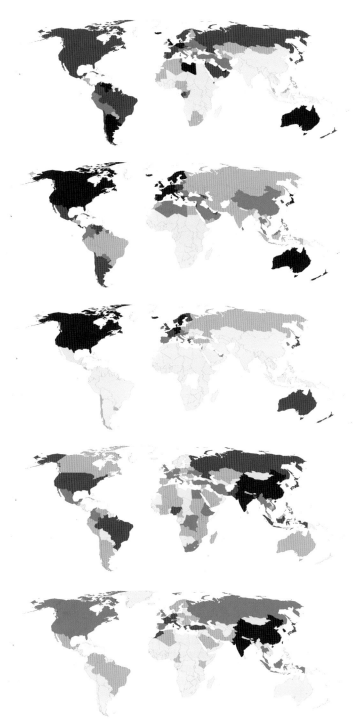

EDUCATION

=

SHOPPING

Source: MUTATIONS
Rem Koolhaas

Reflection: In a world powered by shopping, will the marketplace demand greater opportunities for international mobility and will it transform the values of an international education?

Korea, Republic of

High Income	Republic	Christian 49%	

Population, 2000 (mil)	46.7	GDP per capita (US$)	17,380	HDI rank	27
Percent in EU	12.3	Percent abroad - English	66.9	Percent tertiary abroad	4.3
Est. tertiary enrollment	1,804,545	Num. tertiary institutions	370	Students abroad	76,790

HOST	STUDENTS
United States	45,685
Japan	18,237
Germany	4,853
United Kingdom	2,316
Australia	2,174
All others	3,525

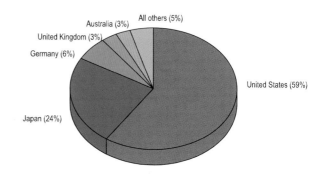

Japan

High Income	Constitutional Monarchy with a parliamentary government	Shinto & Buddhist 84%

Population, 2000 (mil)	127.1	GDP per capita (US$)	26,755	HDI rank	9
Percent in EU	17.4	Percent abroad - English	91.4	Percent tertiary abroad	2.2
Est. tertiary enrollment	2,837,115	Num. tertiary institutions	590	Students abroad	61,637

HOST	STUDENTS
United States	46,497
United Kingdom	6,154
Germany	2,182
Australia	1,762
France	1,446
All others	3,596

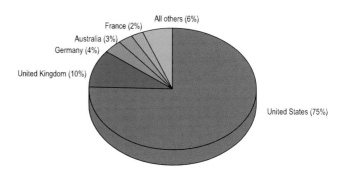

Population, 2000 (mil)	**10.6**	GDP per capita (US$)	**16,501**	HDI rank	**24**
Percent in EU	**91.3**	Percent abroad - English	**59.2**	Percent tertiary abroad	**26.2**
Est. tertiary enrollment	**201,868**	Num. tertiary institutions	**40**	Students abroad	**52,845**

HOST	STUDENTS
United Kingdom	28,250
Italy	8,126
Germany	7,516
United States	2,768
France	2,537
All others	3,648

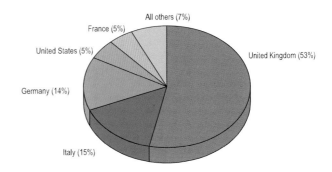

All others (7%)
France (5%)
United States (5%)
Germany (14%)
Italy (15%)
United Kingdom (53%)

Population, 2000 (mil)	**82.0**	GDP per capita (US$)	**25,103**	HDI rank	**17**
Percent in EU	**66.7**	Percent abroad - English	**47.8**	Percent tertiary abroad	**2.5**
Est. tertiary enrollment	**2,117,891**	Num. tertiary institutions	**306**	Students abroad	**52,472**

HOST	STUDENTS
United Kingdom	13,244
United States	10,128
Austria	5,888
Switzerland	5,512
France	5,436
All others	12,264

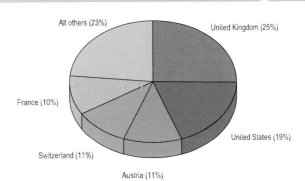

All others (23%)
United Kingdom (25%)
France (10%)
Switzerland (11%)
Austria (11%)
United States (19%)

France

High Income	Republic	Roman Catholic 88%	France

Population, 2000 (mil)	59.2	GDP per capita (US$)	24,223	HDI rank	12
Percent in EU	71.5	Percent abroad - English	47.3	Percent tertiary abroad	2.9
Est. tertiary enrollment	1,751,236	Num. tertiary institutions	480	Students abroad	50,896

HOST	STUDENTS
United Kingdom	12,388
Belgium	9,837
United States	7,273
Germany	6,246
Spain	4,582
All others	10,570

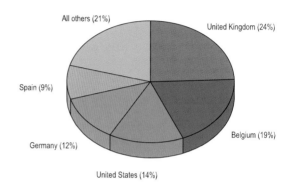

All others (21%); United Kingdom (24%); Spain (9%); Germany (12%); United States (14%); Belgium (19%)

Italy

High Income	Republic	Predominantly Roman Catholic	Italy

Population, 2000 (mil)	57.5	GDP per capita (US$)	23,626	HDI rank	20
Percent in EU	80.6	Percent abroad - English	24.2	Percent tertiary abroad	2.8
Est. tertiary enrollment	1,461,392	Num. tertiary institutions	73	Students abroad	40,728

HOST	STUDENTS
Austria	7,064
Germany	6,771
United Kingdom	5,973
Spain	4,572
Switzerland	4,017
All others	12,331

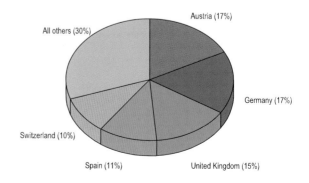

Austria (17%); All others (30%); Germany (17%); Switzerland (10%); United Kingdom (15%); Spain (11%)

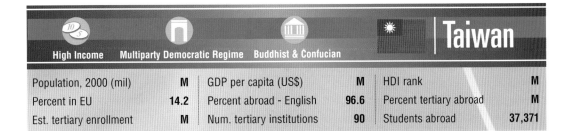

Population, 2000 (mil)	M	GDP per capita (US$)	M	HDI rank	M
Percent in EU	14.2	Percent abroad - English	96.6	Percent tertiary abroad	M
Est. tertiary enrollment	M	Num. tertiary institutions	90	Students abroad	37,371

HOST	STUDENTS
United States	28,566
United Kingdom	4,032
Australia	2,440
Germany	1,265
All others	1,068

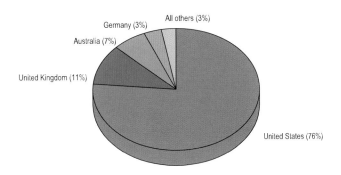

All others (3%)
Germany (3%)
Australia (7%)
United Kingdom (11%)
United States (76%)

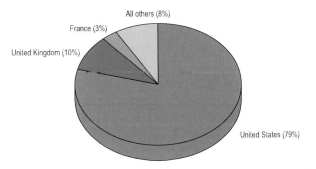

High Income   Confederation with Parliamentary Democracy   Roman Catholic 46%   **Canada**

Population, 2000 (mil)	30.8	GDP per capita (US$)	27,840	HDI rank	3
Percent in EU	17.1	Percent abroad - English	91.6	Percent tertiary abroad	1.5
Est. tertiary enrollment	2,087,101	Num. tertiary institutions	97	Students abroad	31,965

HOST	STUDENTS
United States	25,279
United Kingdom	3,039
France	976
All others	2,671

All others (8%)
France (3%)
United Kingdom (10%)
United States (79%)

United States

High Income	Federal Republic; strong democratic tradition	Protestant 56%

Population, 2000 (mil)	**283.2**	GDP per capita (US$)	**34,142**	HDI rank	**6**
Percent in EU	**71.2**	Percent abroad - English	**65.6**	Percent tertiary abroad	**0.2**
Est. tertiary enrollment	**14,664,817**	Num. tertiary institutions	**1835**	Students abroad	**31,542**

HOST	STUDENTS
United Kingdom	11,553
Canada	3,822
Germany	3,467
Australia	2,846
France	2,515
All others	7,339

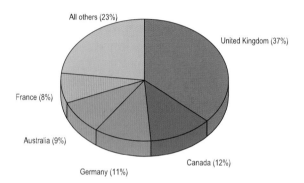

A much larger number of US students abroad is reported in the *Open Doors* report, which includes all students receiving US institution credit for study abroad. Student abroad data used throughout this Atlas refers to students enrolled in host country institutions as reported by those host countries.

Spain

High Income	Parliamentary Monarchy	Roman Catholic 94%

Population, 2000 (mil)	**39.9**	GDP per capita (US$)	**19,472**	HDI rank	**21**
Percent in EU	**77.2**	Percent abroad - English	**44.6**	Percent tertiary abroad	**2.1**
Est. tertiary enrollment	**1,231,568**	Num. tertiary institutions	**77**	Students abroad	**26,182**

HOST	STUDENTS
United Kingdom	7,198
Germany	5,588
United States	4,156
France	3,761
All others	5,479

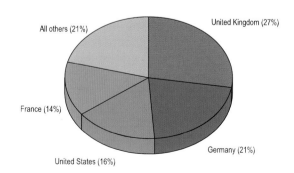

				Hong Kong
High Income	NA	Local Religions 90%		

Population, 2000 (mil)	6.9	GDP per capita (US$)	25,153
Percent in EU	33.2	Percent abroad - English	99.4
Est. tertiary enrollment	95,972	Num. tertiary institutions	19

HDI rank	23
Percent tertiary abroad	26.1
Students abroad	25,073

HOST	STUDENTS
United Kingdom	8,278
United States	7,627
Australia	6,502
Canada	2,176
All others	490

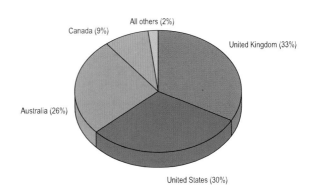

All others (2%)
Canada (9%)
United Kingdom (33%)
Australia (26%)
United States (30%)

				United Kingdom
High Income	Constitutional Monarchy	Anglican & Roman Catholic		

Population, 2000 (mil)	59.4	GDP per capita (US$)	23,509
Percent in EU	51.4	Percent abroad - English	48.2
Est. tertiary enrollment	1,279,772	Num. tertiary institutions	268

HDI rank	13
Percent tertiary abroad	1.7
Students abroad	21,966

HOST	STUDENTS
United States	8,139
France	3,147
Spain	2,660
Germany	2,281
Canada	1,047
All others	4,692

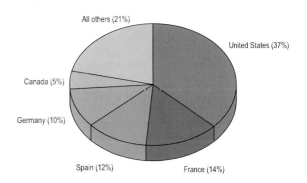

All others (21%)
United States (37%)
Canada (5%)
Germany (10%)
Spain (12%)
France (14%)

Singapore

High Income | Parliamentary Republic | Buddhist

Population, 2000 (mil)	**4.0**	GDP per capita (US$)	**23,356**	HDI rank	**25**
Percent in EU	**26.3**	Percent abroad - English	**98.2**	Percent tertiary abroad	**29.1**
Est. tertiary enrollment	**63,262**	Num. tertiary institutions	**7**	Students abroad	**18,392**

HOST	STUDENTS
Australia	8,647
United Kingdom	4,625
United States	4,166
All others	954

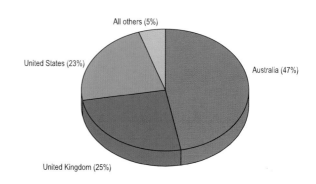

All others (5%)
United States (23%)
Australia (47%)
United Kingdom (25%)

Ireland

High Income | Republic | Roman Catholic 92%

Population, 2000 (mil)	**3.8**	GDP per capita (US$)	**29,866**	HDI rank	**18**
Percent in EU	**91.0**	Percent abroad - English	**88.2**	Percent tertiary abroad	**16.2**
Est. tertiary enrollment	**94,303**	Num. tertiary institutions	**42**	Students abroad	**15,300**

HOST	STUDENTS
United Kingdom	12,184
United States	1,086
France	594
Germany	536
All others	900

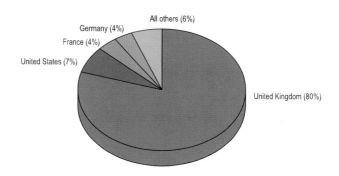

All others (6%)
Germany (4%)
France (4%)
United States (7%)
United Kingdom (80%)

Sweden

High Income	**Constitutional Monarchy**	**Lutheran 87%**			

Population, 2000 (mil)	**8.8**	GDP per capita (US$)	**24,277**	HDI rank	**2**
Percent in EU	**54.2**	Percent abroad - English	**73.0**	Percent tertiary abroad	**6.8**
Est. tertiary enrollment	**199,260**	Num. tertiary institutions	**52**	Students abroad	**13,628**

HOST	STUDENTS
United States	4,598
United Kingdom	3,977
France	952
Australia	916
Germany	881
All others	2,304

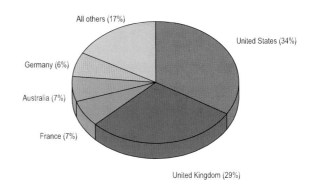

All others (17%) · United States (34%) · Germany (6%) · Australia (7%) · France (7%) · United Kingdom (29%)

Norway

High Income	**Constitutional Monarchy**	**Evangelical Lutheran 86%**			

Population, 2000 (mil)	**4.5**	GDP per capita (US$)	**29,918**	HDI rank	**1**
Percent in EU	**65.8**	Percent abroad - English	**64.6**	Percent tertiary abroad	**8.6**
Est. tertiary enrollment	**147,706**	Num. tertiary institutions	**43**	Students abroad	**12,708**

HOST	STUDENTS
United Kingdom	3,861
United States	2,098
Australia	1,881
Denmark	1,293
Sweden	1,214
All others	2,361

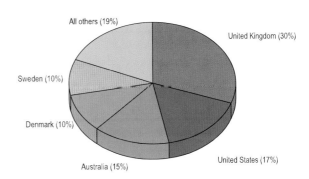

All others (19%) · United Kingdom (30%) · Sweden (10%) · Denmark (10%) · Australia (15%) · United States (17%)

Netherlands

High Income	Constitutional Monarchy	Roman Catholic 31%	

Population, 2000 (mil)	**15.9**	GDP per capita (US$)	**25,657**	HDI rank	**8**
Percent in EU	**79.1**	Percent abroad - English	**39.0**	Percent tertiary abroad	**2.4**
Est. tertiary enrollment	**500,116**	Num. tertiary institutions	**79**	Students abroad	**11,768**

HOST	STUDENTS
Belgium	2,692
United Kingdom	2,440
United States	1,856
Germany	1,770
Spain	941
All others	2,069

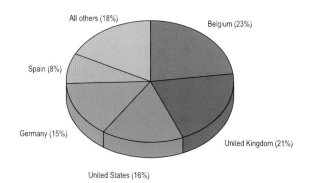

All others (18%)
Belgium (23%)
Spain (8%)
Germany (15%)
United States (16%)
United Kingdom (21%)

Austria

High Income	Federal Republic	Roman Catholic 78%	

Population, 2000 (mil)	**8.1**	GDP per capita (US$)	**26,765**	HDI rank	**15**
Percent in EU	**81.9**	Percent abroad - English	**22.3**	Percent tertiary abroad	**5.1**
Est. tertiary enrollment	**216,243**	Num. tertiary institutions	**59**	Students abroad	**11,012**

HOST	STUDENTS
Germany	6,127
United Kingdom	1,226
United States	1,062
Switzerland	728
All others	1,869

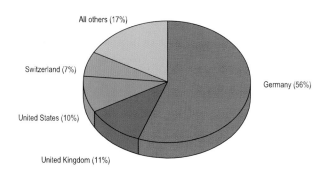

All others (17%)
Switzerland (7%)
United States (10%)
United Kingdom (11%)
Germany (56%)

Portugal

High Income — **Parliamentary Democracy** — **Roman Catholic 94%**

Population, 2000 (mil)	10.0	GDP per capita (US$)	17,290	HDI rank	28
Percent in EU	85.8	Percent abroad - English	32.2	Percent tertiary abroad	5.5
Est. tertiary enrollment	185,640	Num. tertiary institutions	152	Students abroad	10,109

HOST	STUDENTS
France	3,041
United Kingdom	2,255
Germany	1,527
Spain	900
United States	884
All others	1,938

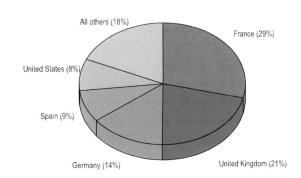

France (29%), United Kingdom (21%), Germany (14%), Spain (9%), United States (8%), All others (18%)

Belgium

High Income — **Federal Parliamentary Democracy under a constitutional monarch** — **Roman Catholic 75%**

Population, 2000 (mil)	10.2	GDP per capita (US$)	27,178	HDI rank	4
Percent in EU	86.1	Percent abroad - English	35.9	Percent tertiary abroad	3.5
Est. tertiary enrollment	281,126	Num. tertiary institutions	248	Students abroad	9,737

HOST	STUDENTS
United Kingdom	2,389
France	1,938
Netherlands	1,373
Spain	1,250
Germany	923
All others	1,864

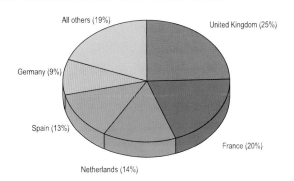

United Kingdom (25%), France (20%), Netherlands (14%), Spain (13%), Germany (9%), All others (19%)

Cyprus

High Income	Republic	Greek Orthodox 78%	

Population, 2000 (mil)	0.8	GDP per capita (US$)	20,824	HDI rank	26
Percent in EU	43.4	Percent abroad - English	63.1	Percent tertiary abroad	128.2
Est. tertiary enrollment	7,340	Num. tertiary institutions	7	Students abroad	9,413

HOST	STUDENTS
United Kingdom	3,664
Turkey	3,053
United States	2,217
All others	479

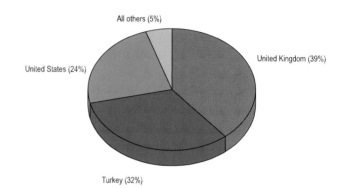

All others (5%)
United States (24%)
United Kingdom (39%)
Turkey (32%)

Finland

High Income	Republic	Evangelical Lutheran 89%	

Population, 2000 (mil)	5.2	GDP per capita (US$)	24,996	HDI rank	10
Percent in EU	87.6	Percent abroad - English	38.8	Percent tertiary abroad	5.4
Est. tertiary enrollment	170,887	Num. tertiary institutions	54	Students abroad	9,238

HOST	STUDENTS
Sweden	3,368
United Kingdom	2,503
Germany	998
United States	893
All others	1,476

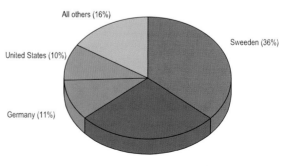

All others (16%)
United States (10%)
Sweeden (36%)
Germany (11%)
United Kingdom (27%)

Switzerland

High Income	Federal Republic	Roman Catholic 46%		

Population, 2000 (mil)	7.2	GDP per capita (US$)	28,769	HDI rank	11
Percent in EU	72.1	Percent abroad - English	45.0	Percent tertiary abroad	5.5
Est. tertiary enrollment	145,870	Num. tertiary institutions	24	Students abroad	8,027

HOST	STUDENTS
United States	1,850
Germany	1,763
United Kingdom	1,393
France	978
Italy	743
All others	1,300

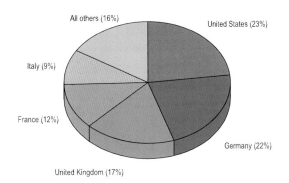

Israel

High Income	Parliamentary Democracy	Jewish 80%		

Population, 2000 (mil)	6.0	GDP per capita (US$)	20,131	HDI rank	22
Percent in EU	46.0	Percent abroad - English	65.5	Percent tertiary abroad	4.5
Est. tertiary enrollment	169,588	Num. tertiary institutions	38	Students abroad	7,575

HOST	STUDENTS
United States	3,402
United Kingdom	1,397
Germany	876
Italy	626
All others	1,274

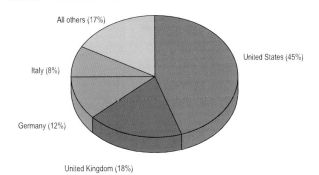

Luxembourg

High Income	Constitutional Monarchy	Roman Catholic 87%	

Population, 2000 (mil)	0.4	GDP per capita (US$)	50,061	HDI rank	16
Percent in EU	95.1	Percent abroad - English	13.9	Percent tertiary abroad	M
Est. tertiary enrollment	M	Num. tertiary institutions	4	Students abroad	5,686

HOST	STUDENTS
Germany	1,605
Belgium	1,468
France	1,250
United Kingdom	688
All others	675

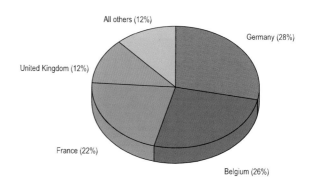

All others (12%)
Germany (28%)
United Kingdom (12%)
France (22%)
Belgium (26%)

Australia

High Income	Democratic, Federal-State System	Anglican 26%	

Population, 2000 (mil)	19.1	GDP per capita (US$)	25,693	HDI rank	5
Percent in EU	37.0	Percent abroad - English	78.5	Percent tertiary abroad	1.1
Est. tertiary enrollment	526,524	Num. tertiary institutions	81	Students abroad	5,524

HOST	STUDENTS
United States	2,645
United Kingdom	1,235
Canada	380
Japan	355
All others	909

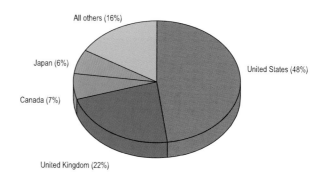

All others (16%)
Japan (6%)
United States (48%)
Canada (7%)
United Kingdom (22%)

Selected countries with populations projected to decrease between 2000 and 2050

Russian Federation	-30.3
Italy	-22.0
Switzerland	-19.0
Poland	-14.7
Japan	-13.6
Greece	-10.0
Portugal	-9.9
Austria	-9.0
Spain	-8.4
Germany	-3.8

Source: United Nations Population Division

Reflection: Over the next 50 years, global demographic changes will remake the balance of power in the world.

Malaysia

Upper Mid Income	Constitutional Monarchy	Muslim		
Population, 2000 (mil)	22.2	GDP per capita (US$)	9,068	HDI rank	59
Percent in EU	30.7	Percent abroad - English	89.2	Percent tertiary abroad	23.1
Est. tertiary enrollment	142,684	Num. tertiary institutions	27	Students abroad	32,958

HOST	STUDENTS
Australia	9,866
United Kingdom	9,168
United States	7,795
Japan	1,956
Jordan	1,232
All others	2,941

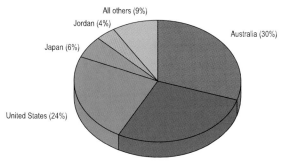

Poland

Upper Mid Income	Republic	Roman Catholic 95%		
Population, 2000 (mil)	38.6	GDP per capita (US$)	9,051	HDI rank	37
Percent in EU	83.0	Percent abroad - English	18.3	Percent tertiary abroad	3.2
Est. tertiary enrollment	552,923	Num. tertiary institutions	258	Students abroad	17,517

HOST	STUDENTS
Germany	9,328
United States	2,432
France	1,854
All others	3,903

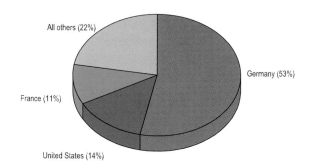

Brazil

Upper Mid Income		Federal Republic		Roman Catholic 80%	

Population, 2000 (mil)	170.4	GDP per capita (US$)	7,625	HDI rank	73
Percent in EU	40.6	Percent abroad - English	62.3	Percent tertiary abroad	1.0
Est. tertiary enrollment	1,769,597	Num. tertiary institutions	1065	Students abroad	16,756

HOST	STUDENTS
United States	8,846
Germany	1,432
France	1,380
Portugal	1,338
Spain	1,102
United Kingdom	1,055
All others	1,603

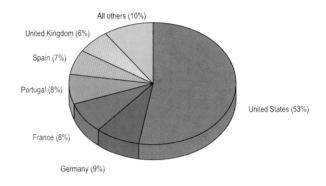

All others (10%), United Kingdom (6%), Spain (7%), Portugal (8%), France (8%), Germany (9%), United States (53%)

Mexico

Upper Mid Income		Federal Republic		Roman Catholic 89%	

Population, 2000 (mil)	98.9	GDP per capita (US$)	9,023	HDI rank	54
Percent in EU	23.6	Percent abroad - English	84.4	Percent tertiary abroad	1.0
Est. tertiary enrollment	1,484,926	Num. tertiary institutions	784	Students abroad	15,264

HOST	STUDENTS
United States	10,670
Spain	1,445
United Kingdom	1,400
Canada	726
All others	1,023

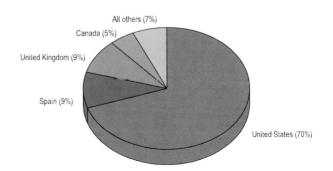

All others (7%), Canada (5%), United Kingdom (9%), Spain (9%), United States (70%)

Saudi Arabia

Upper Mid Income	Monarchy	Muslim 100%	

Population, 2000 (mil)	20.3	GDP per capita (US$)	11,367	HDI rank	71
Percent in EU	20.1	Percent abroad - English	87.8	Percent tertiary abroad	4.4
Est. tertiary enrollment	186,998	Num. tertiary institutions	8	Students abroad	8,288

HOST	STUDENTS
United States	5,273
United Kingdom	1,519
Jordan	775
Canada	426
All others	295

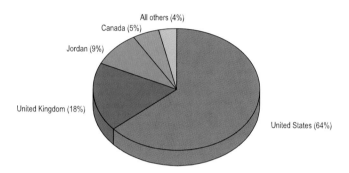

Venezuela

Upper Mid Income	Federal Republic	Roman Catholic 96%	

Population, 2000 (mil)	24.2	GDP per capita (US$)	5,794	HDI rank	69
Percent in EU	32.0	Percent abroad - English	71.2	Percent tertiary abroad	1.3
Est. tertiary enrollment	642,311	Num. tertiary institutions	249	Students abroad	8,053

HOST	STUDENTS
United States	5,217
Spain	1,094
Portugal	467
All others	1,275

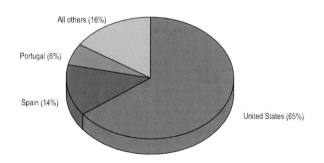

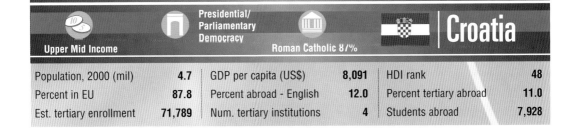

Croatia

Upper Mid Income	Presidential/ Parliamentary Democracy	Roman Catholic 87%	

Population, 2000 (mil)	4.7	GDP per capita (US$)	8,091	HDI rank	48
Percent in EU	87.8	Percent abroad - English	12.0	Percent tertiary abroad	11.0
Est. tertiary enrollment	71,789	Num. tertiary institutions	4	Students abroad	7,928

HOST	STUDENTS
Germany	4,614
Italy	1,011
Austria	827
United States	782
All others	694

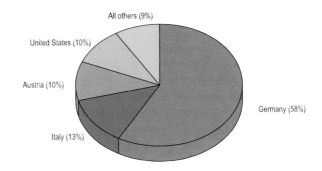

All others (9%)
United States (10%)
Austria (10%)
Germany (58%)
Italy (13%)

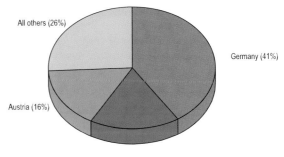

Hungary

Upper Mid Income	Parliamentary Democracy	Roman Catholic 67%

Population, 2000 (mil)	10.0	GDP per capita (US$)	12,416	HDI rank	35
Percent in EU	78.5	Percent abroad - English	23.9	Percent tertiary abroad	6.8
Est. tertiary enrollment	100,341	Num. tertiary institutions	59	Students abroad	6,788

HOST	STUDENTS
Germany	2,779
United States	1,174
Austria	1,092
All others	1,743

All others (26%)
Germany (41%)
Austria (16%)
United States (17%)

Population, 2000 (mil)	37.0	GDP per capita (US$)	12,377	HDI rank	34
Percent in EU	47.5	Percent abroad - English	56.0	Percent tertiary abroad	0.6
Est. tertiary enrollment	1,090,819	Num. tertiary institutions	97	Students abroad	6,676

HOST	STUDENTS
United States	3,172
Spain	1,537
France	471
All others	1,496

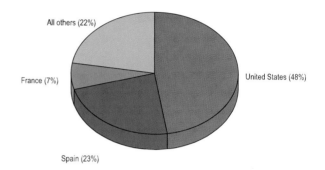

All others (22%)
France (7%)
United States (48%)
Spain (23%)

Population, 2000 (mil)	3.5	GDP per capita (US$)	4,308	HDI rank	75
Percent in EU	60.2	Percent abroad - English	39.6	Percent tertiary abroad	6.4
Est. tertiary enrollment	102,965	Num. tertiary institutions	24	Students abroad	6,554

HOST	STUDENTS
France	2,500
United States	2,005
Germany	487
All others	1,562

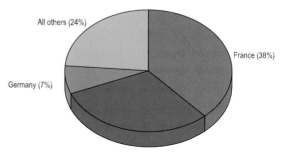

All others (24%)
Germany (7%)
France (38%)
United States (31%)

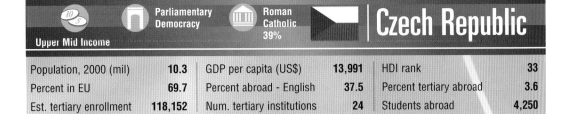

Czech Republic

Upper Mid Income	Parliamentary Democracy	Roman Catholic 39%		
Population, 2000 (mil)	10.3	GDP per capita (US$)	13,991	HDI rank	33
Percent in EU	69.7	Percent abroad - English	37.5	Percent tertiary abroad	3.6
Est. tertiary enrollment	118,152	Num. tertiary institutions	24	Students abroad	4,250

HOST	STUDENTS
Germany	1,640
United States	1,112
United Kingdom	409
All others	1,089

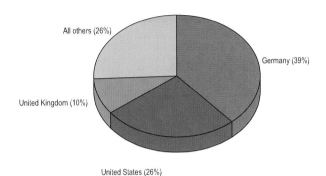

Chile

Upper Mid Income	Republic	Roman Catholic 89%		
Population, 2000 (mil)	15.2	GDP per capita (US$)	9,417	HDI rank	38
Percent in EU	56.9	Percent abroad - English	48.0	Percent tertiary abroad	1.4
Est. tertiary enrollment	287,381	Num. tertiary institutions	159	Students abroad	4,115

HOST	STUDENTS
United States	1,553
Spain	764
Germany	459
All others	1,339

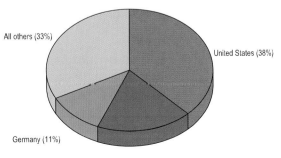

The global demand
for higher education is
forecast to increase
from 97 million in 2000
to 263 million in 2025.

Source: Global Student Mobility 2025
IDP Education Australia

*Reflection: Currently, the largest part of
existing higher education capacity globally is
not centered in parts of the world that will
experience substantial growth over the next
20 years.*

LOWER MID INCOME LISTED BY STUDENTS ABROAD

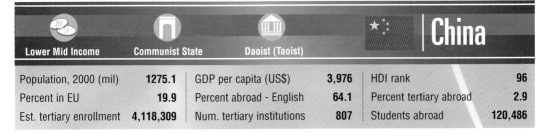

Lower Mid Income | **Communist State** | **Daoist (Taoist)** | | **China**

Population, 2000 (mil)	1275.1	GDP per capita (US$)	3,976	HDI rank	96
Percent in EU	19.9	Percent abroad - English	64.1	Percent tertiary abroad	2.9
Est. tertiary enrollment	4,118,309	Num. tertiary institutions	807	Students abroad	120,486

HOST	STUDENTS
United States	59,939
Japan	28,076
United Kingdom	10,332
Germany	9,109
Australia	3,712
All others	9,318

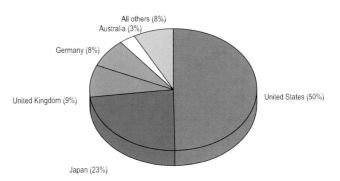

All others (8%)
Australia (3%)
Germany (8%)
United Kingdom (9%)
United States (50%)
Japan (23%)

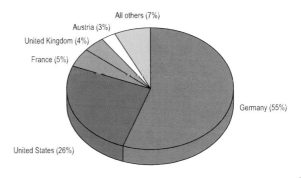

Lower Mid Income | **Republican Parliamentary Democracy** | **Muslim 99%** | | **Turkey**

Population, 2000 (mil)	66.7	GDP per capita (US$)	6,974	HDI rank	85
Percent in EU	72.1	Percent abroad - English	30.5	Percent tertiary abroad	5.0
Est. tertiary enrollment	847,698	Num. tertiary institutions	56	Students abroad	42,690

HOST	STUDENTS
Germany	23,640
United States	10,983
France	2,140
United Kingdom	1,764
Austria	1,172
All others	2,991

All others (7%)
Austria (3%)
United Kingdom (4%)
France (5%)
Germany (55%)
United States (26%)

Morocco

Population, 2000 (mil)	29.9	GDP per capita (US$)	3,546	HDI rank	123
Percent in EU	92.3	Percent abroad - English	7.0	Percent tertiary abroad	14.4
Est. tertiary enrollment	287,185	Num. tertiary institutions	133	Students abroad	41,296

HOST	STUDENTS
France	21,048
Germany	6,204
Belgium	5,355
Spain	3,144
All others	5,545

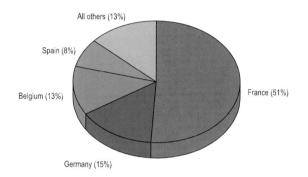

Kazakhstan

Population, 2000 (mil)	16.2	GDP per capita (US$)	5,871	HDI rank	79
Percent in EU	3.4	Percent abroad - English	3.4	Percent tertiary abroad	4.0
Est. tertiary enrollment	525,573	Num. tertiary institutions	54	Students abroad	20,938

HOST	STUDENTS
Russia	18,486
Turkey	1,142
United States	540
All others	770

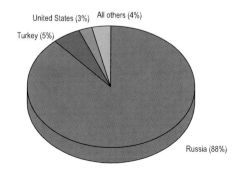

				Russia
Lower Mid Income	**Federation**	**Russian Orthodox**		

Population, 2000 (mil)	**145.5**	GDP per capita (US$)	**8,377**	HDI rank	**60**
Percent in EU	**55.7**	Percent abroad - English	**42.7**	Percent tertiary abroad	**0.4**
Est. tertiary enrollment	**5,077,890**	Num. tertiary institutions	**703**	Students abroad	**20,160**

HOST	STUDENTS
Germany	6,987
United States	6,858
France	1,453
United Kingdom	1,358
Turkey	1,004
All others	2,500

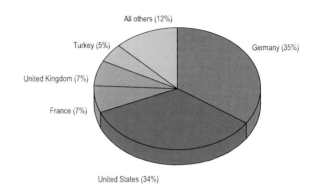

				Thailand
Lower Mid Income	**Republic under transition to multiparty democratic rule**	**Buddhism 95%**		

Population, 2000 (mil)	**62.8**	GDP per capita (US$)	**6,402**	HDI rank	**70**
Percent in EU	**19.0**	Percent abroad - English	**89.0**	Percent tertiary abroad	**M**
Est. tertiary enrollment	**M**	Num. tertiary institutions	**94**	Students abroad	**19,232**

HOST	STUDENTS
United States	11,187
Australia	2,716
United Kingdom	2,704
Japan	1,019
All others	1,606

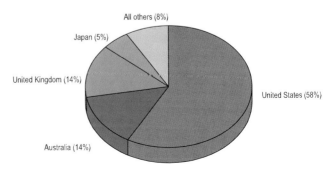

Algeria

Lower Mid Income		Republic		Sunni Muslim 99%	
Population, 2000 (mil)	30.3	GDP per capita (US$)	5,308	HDI rank	106
Percent in EU	95.9	Percent abroad - English	4.1	Percent tertiary abroad	4.6
Est. tertiary enrollment	337,149	Num. tertiary institutions	24	Students abroad	15,531

HOST	STUDENTS
France	13,539
Belgium	412
Germany	346
All others	1,234

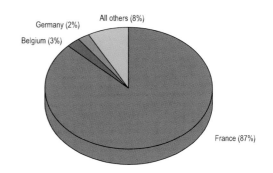

Iran

Lower Mid Income		Theocratic Republic		Shi'a Muslim 89%	
Population, 2000 (mil)	70.3	GDP per capita (US$)	5,884	HDI rank	98
Percent in EU	77.7	Percent abroad - English	22.4	Percent tertiary abroad	2.4
Est. tertiary enrollment	604,918	Num. tertiary institutions	98	Students abroad	14,436

HOST	STUDENTS
Germany	6,359
United States	1,844
France	1,379
United Kingdom	836
Austria	768
All others	3,250

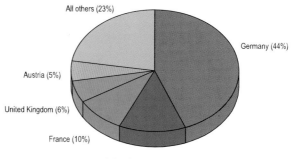

Bulgaria

Lower Mid Income · **Parliamentary Democracy** · **Bulgarian Orthodox 84%**

Population, 2000 (mil)	7.9	GDP per capita (US$)	5,710	HDI rank	62
Percent in EU	67.8	Percent abroad - English	28.5	Percent tertiary abroad	7.2
Est. tertiary enrollment	181,457	Num. tertiary institutions	37	Students abroad	13,104

HOST	STUDENTS
Germany	5,015
United States	3,270
France	1,579
Austria	1,370
Turkey	615
All others	1,255

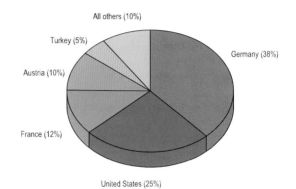

All others (10%)
Turkey (5%)
Germany (38%)
Austria (10%)
France (12%)
United States (25%)

Colombia

Lower Mid Income · **Republic** · **Roman Catholic 90%**

Population, 2000 (mil)	42.1	GDP per capita (US$)	6,248	HDI rank	68
Percent in EU	31.2	Percent abroad - English	70.6	Percent tertiary abroad	1.9
Est. tertiary enrollment	558,199	Num. tertiary institutions	158	Students abroad	10,735

HOST	STUDENTS
United States	6,765
Spain	1,156
France	884
Germany	544
United Kingdom	403
All others	983

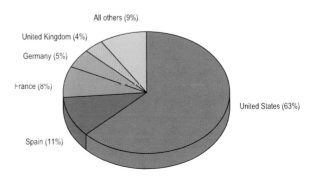

All others (9%)
United Kingdom (4%)
Germany (5%)
France (8%)
United States (63%)
Spain (11%)

Romania

Lower Mid Income		Republic		Eastern Orthodox 87%	

Population, 2000 (mil)	22.4	GDP per capita (US$)	6,423	HDI rank	63
Percent in EU	64.9	Percent abroad - English	35.6	Percent tertiary abroad	5.4
Est. tertiary enrollment	187,382	Num. tertiary institutions	49	Students abroad	10,198

HOST	STUDENTS
United States	2,976
France	2,271
Germany	2,232
United Kingdom	455
All others	2,264

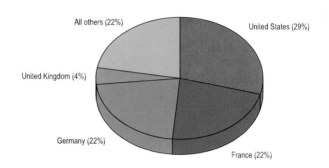

Serbia & Montenegro

Lower Mid Income		Republic		Orthodox 65%	

Population, 2000 (mil)	M	GDP per capita (US$)	M	HDI rank	M
Percent in EU	73.0	Percent abroad - English	26.2	Percent tertiary abroad	6.0
Est. tertiary enrollment	138,377	Num. tertiary institutions	7	Students abroad	8,358

HOST	STUDENTS
Germany	3,570
United States	1,790
Austria	949
France	444
All others	1,605

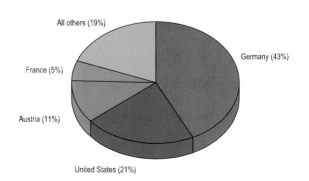

Egypt

Lower Mid Income	Republic	Muslim 94%

Population, 2000 (mil)	67.9	GDP per capita (US$)	3,635	HDI rank	115
Percent in EU	55.0	Percent abroad - English	58.8	Percent tertiary abroad	0.7
Est. tertiary enrollment	941,189	Num. tertiary institutions	42	Students abroad	6,150

HOST	STUDENTS
United States	2,255
Germany	1,191
United Kingdom	1,186
France	555
All others	963

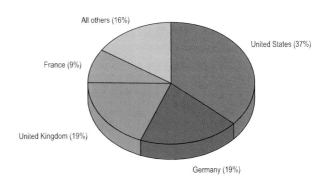

All others (16%)
United States (37%)
France (9%)
United Kingdom (19%)
Germany (19%)

Peru

Lower Mid Income	Constitutional Republic	Roman Catholic 90%

Population, 2000 (mil)	25.7	GDP per capita (US$)	4,799	HDI rank	82
Percent in EU	48.0	Percent abroad - English	50.1	Percent tertiary abroad	0.8
Est. tertiary enrollment	770,241	Num. tertiary institutions	47	Students abroad	5,748

HOST	STUDENTS
United States	2,660
Spain	1,083
Germany	797
All others	1,208

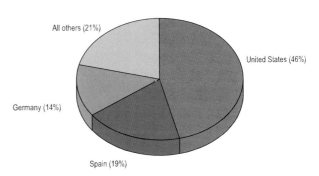

All others (21%)
United States (46%)
Germany (14%)
Spain (19%)

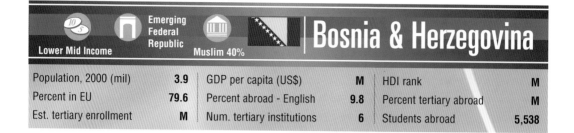

Bosnia & Herzegovina

Lower Mid Income | Emerging Federal Republic | Muslim 40%

Population, 2000 (mil)	3.9	GDP per capita (US$)	M	HDI rank	M
Percent in EU	79.6	Percent abroad - English	9.8	Percent tertiary abroad	M
Est. tertiary enrollment	M	Num. tertiary institutions	6	Students abroad	5,538

HOST	STUDENTS
Germany	1,889
Austria	732
Sweden	665
Denmark	541
Turkey	533
All others	1,178

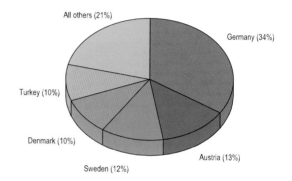

All others (21%)
Germany (34%)
Turkey (10%)
Denmark (10%)
Sweden (12%)
Austria (13%)

Belarus

Lower Mid Income | Republic | Eastern Orthodox 80%

Population, 2000 (mil)	10.2	GDP per capita (US$)	7,544	HDI rank	56
Percent in EU	20.4	Percent abroad - English	7.3	Percent tertiary abroad	1.6
Est. tertiary enrollment	338,271	Num. tertiary institutions	35	Students abroad	5,288

HOST	STUDENTS
Russia	3,868
Germany	754
United States	311
All others	355

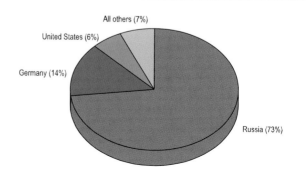

All others (7%)
United States (6%)
Germany (14%)
Russia (73%)

Sri Lanka

Lower Mid Income	Republic	Buddhist 70%

Population, 2000 (mil)	18.9	GDP per capita (US$)	3,530	HDI rank	89
Percent in EU	32.7	Percent abroad - English	87.2	Percent tertiary abroad	6.5
Est. tertiary enrollment	80,406	Num. tertiary institutions	16	Students abroad	5,249

HOST	STUDENTS
United States	1,964
United Kingdom	1,334
Australia	1,065
Japan	278
All others	608

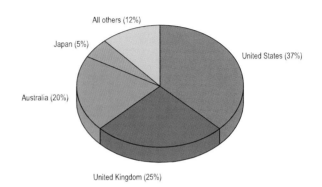

Syria

Lower Mid Income	Republic under military regime since March 1963	Sunni Muslim 74%

Population, 2000 (mil)	16.2	GDP per capita (US$)	3,556	HDI rank	108
Percent in EU	57.1	Percent abroad - English	19.6	Percent tertiary abroad	1.9
Est. tertiary enrollment	267,420	Num. tertiary institutions	5	Students abroad	5,088

HOST	STUDENTS
France	1,322
Jordan	1,160
Germany	922
United States	713
All others	971

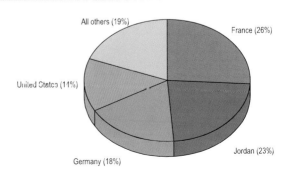

Philippines

Lower Mid Income	Republic	Roman Catholic 83%

Population, 2000 (mil)	75.7	GDP per capita (US$)	3,971	HDI rank	77
Percent in EU	14.7	Percent abroad - English	80.8	Percent tertiary abroad	0.3
Est. tertiary enrollment	2,012,183	Num. tertiary institutions	1329	Students abroad	5,013

HOST	STUDENTS
United States	3,139
Australia	478
Japan	430
All others	966

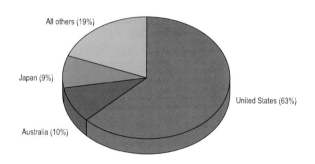

All others (19%)
Japan (9%)
United States (63%)
Australia (10%)

Jordan

Lower Mid Income	Constitutional Monarchy	Sunni Muslim 92%

Population, 2000 (mil)	4.9	GDP per capita (US$)	3,966	HDI rank	99
Percent in EU	46.2	Percent abroad - English	64.4	Percent tertiary abroad	M
Est. tertiary enrollment	M	Num. tertiary institutions	21	Students abroad	4,975

HOST	STUDENTS
United States	2,187
Germany	1,029
United Kingdom	810
Turkey	268
All others	681

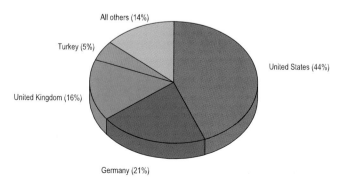

All others (14%)
Turkey (5%)
United States (44%)
United Kingdom (16%)
Germany (21%)

Albania

Lower Mid Income	Emerging Democracy	Muslim 70%	

Population, 2000 (mil)	3.1	GDP per capita (US$)	3,506	HDI rank	92
Percent in EU	62.4	Percent abroad - English	24.9	Percent tertiary abroad	23.4
Est. tertiary enrollment	21,016	Num. tertiary institutions	10	Students abroad	4,919

HOST	STUDENTS
Italy	2,127
United States	1,118
Turkey	558
Germany	407
All others	709

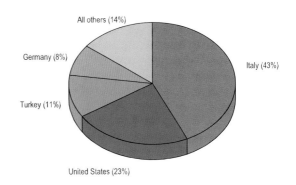

All others (14%)
Germany (8%)
Italy (43%)
Turkey (11%)
United States (23%)

Jamaica

Lower Mid Income	Constitutional Parliamentary Democracy	Protestant 61%	

Population, 2000 (mil)	2.6	GDP per capita (US$)	3,639	HDI rank	86
Percent in EU	8.6	Percent abroad - English	99.1	Percent tertiary abroad	28.0
Est. tertiary enrollment	17,008	Num. tertiary institutions	5	Students abroad	4,761

HOST	STUDENTS
United States	4,225
United Kingdom	369
All others	167

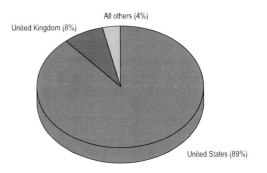

All others (4%)
United Kingdom (8%)
United States (89%)

South Africa

Lower Mid Income | Republic | Christian 68%

Population, 2000 (mil)	43.3	GDP per capita (US$)	9,401	HDI rank	107
Percent in EU	41.0	Percent abroad - English	89.9	Percent tertiary abroad	0.8
Est. tertiary enrollment	500,392	Num. tertiary institutions	85	Students abroad	4,199

HOST	STUDENTS
United States	2,106
United Kingdom	1,291
Australia	252
All others	550

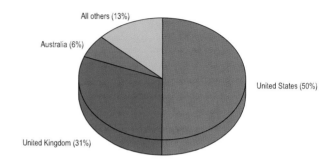

All others (13%)
Australia (6%)
United States (50%)
United Kingdom (31%)

LOW INCOME LISTED BY STUDENTS ABROAD

India

Low Income | Federal Republic | Hindu 81%

Population, 2000 (mil)	1,008.9	GDP per capita (US$)	2,358	HDI rank	124
Percent in EU	9.6	Percent abroad - English	96.4	Percent tertiary abroad	1.2
Est. tertiary enrollment	5,623,237	Num. tertiary institutions	234	Students abroad	66,587

HOST	STUDENTS
United States	54,664
Australia	4,374
United Kingdom	4,241
Germany	1,412
Canada	745
All others	1,151

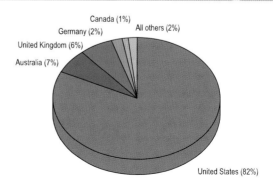

Canada (1%)
Germany (2%)
All others (2%)
United Kingdom (6%)
Australia (7%)
United States (82%)

Indonesia

Population, 2000 (mil)	212.1	GDP per capita (US$)	3,043	HDI rank	110
Percent in EU	14.6	Percent abroad - English	84.6	Percent tertiary abroad	1.4
Est. tertiary enrollment	1,891,434	Num. tertiary institutions	1340	Students abroad	26,833

HOST	STUDENTS
United States	11,625
Australia	9,283
Germany	2,128
Japan	1,143
United Kingdom	1,049
All others	1,605

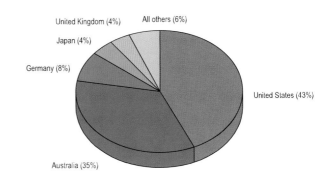

United Kingdom (4%)   All others (6%)
Japan (4%)
Germany (8%)
United States (43%)
Australia (35%)

Ukraine

Population, 2000 (mil)	49.6	GDP per capita (US$)	3,816	HDI rank	80
Percent in EU	35.4	Percent abroad - English	17.5	Percent tertiary abroad	0.8
Est. tertiary enrollment	1,625,303	Num. tertiary institutions	292	Students abroad	13,445

HOST	STUDENTS
Russia	6,272
Germany	3,688
United States	1,909
All others	1,576

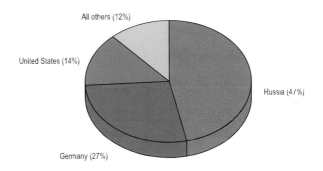

All others (12%)
United States (14%)
Russia (47%)
Germany (27%)

Low Income	**Federal Republic**	**Muslim 97%**	**Pakistan**

Population, 2000 (mil)	141.3	GDP per capita (US$)	1,928	HDI rank	138
Percent in EU	25.7	Percent abroad - English	89.4	Percent tertiary abroad	2.7
Est. tertiary enrollment	419,177	Num. tertiary institutions	45	Students abroad	11,192

HOST	STUDENTS
United States	6,948
United Kingdom	1,911
Australia	673
Germany	653
All others	1,007

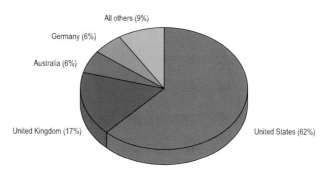

Low Income	**Unitary Republic; multiparty presidential regime**	**Indigenous beliefs 40%**	**Cameroon**

Population, 2000 (mil)	14.9	GDP per capita (US$)	1,703	HDI rank	135
Percent in EU	87.8	Percent abroad - English	12.4	Percent tertiary abroad	25.7
Est. tertiary enrollment	40,240	Num. tertiary institutions	23	Students abroad	10,330

HOST	STUDENTS
Germany	4,141
France	3,279
United States	870
Belgium	705
Italy	665
All others	670

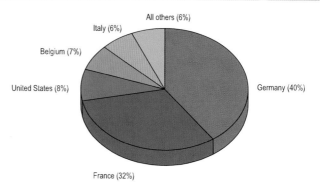

			Kenya
Low Income	Republic	Protestant 45%	

Population, 2000 (mil)	30.7	GDP per capita (US$)	1,022	HDI rank	134
Percent in EU	29.3	Percent abroad - English	93.9	Percent tertiary abroad	24.6
Est. tertiary enrollment	40,393	Num. tertiary institutions	10	Students abroad	9,952

HOST	STUDENTS
United States	6,229
United Kingdom	2,435
Australia	376
All others	912

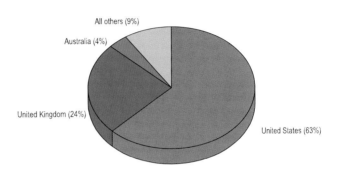

			Nigeria
Low Income	Republic transitioning from military to civilian rule	Muslim 50%	

Population, 2000 (mil)	113.9	GDP per capita (US$)	896	HDI rank	148
Percent in EU	45.9	Percent abroad - English	84.1	Percent tertiary abroad	M
Est. tertiary enrollment	M	Num. tertiary institutions	67	Students abroad	7,555

HOST	STUDENTS
United States	3,820
United Kingdom	2,322
Germany	667
All others	746

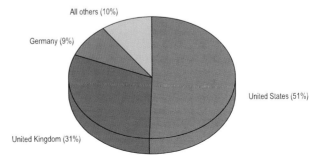

Vietnam

Population, 2000 (mil)	78.1	GDP per capita (US$)	1,996	HDI rank	109
Percent in EU	43.2	Percent abroad - English	49.6	Percent tertiary abroad	4.9
Est. tertiary enrollment	148,191	Num. tertiary institutions	50	Students abroad	7,306

HOST	STUDENTS
United States	2,022
Germany	1,410
Australia	1,257
France	1,226
Japan	531
All others	860

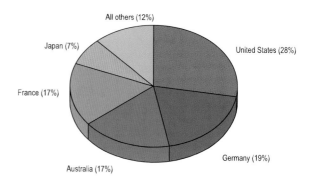

United States (28%)
Germany (19%)
Australia (17%)
France (17%)
Japan (7%)
All others (12%)

Bangladesh

Population, 2000 (mil)	137.4	GDP per capita (US$)	1,602	HDI rank	145
Percent in EU	15.3	Percent abroad - English	83.0	Percent tertiary abroad	1.4
Est. tertiary enrollment	486,921	Num. tertiary institutions	16	Students abroad	6,763

HOST	STUDENTS
United States	4,114
Japan	760
United Kingdom	674
Australia	631
All others	584

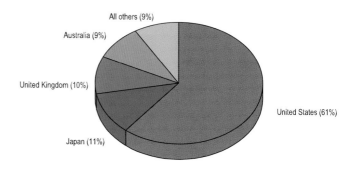

United States (61%)
Japan (11%)
United Kingdom (10%)
Australia (9%)
All others (9%)

Niger

Population, 2000 (mil)	10.8	GDP per capita (US$)	746	HDI rank	172
Percent in EU	95.6	Percent abroad - English	2.2	Percent tertiary abroad	117.4
Est. tertiary enrollment	5,663	Num. tertiary institutions	7	Students abroad	6,646

HOST	STUDENTS
France	6,268
Switzerland	157
All others	221

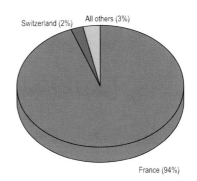

Switzerland (2%) All others (3%)

France (94%)

Somalia

Population, 2000 (mil)	M	GDP per capita (US$)	M	HDI rank	M
Percent in EU	93.9	Percent abroad - English	5.0	Percent tertiary abroad	M
Est. tertiary enrollment	M	Num. tertiary institutions	1	Students abroad	4,854

HOST	STUDENTS
France	4,079
Sweden	172
Switzerland	102
All others	501

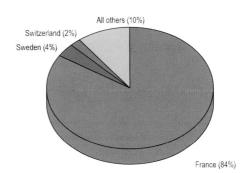

All others (10%)
Switzerland (2%)
Sweden (4%)

France (84%)

Congo, DPR

Low Income | **Dictatorship** | **Roman Catholic 50%**

Population, 2000 (mil)	50.9	GDP per capita (US$)	765	HDI rank	155
Percent in EU	87.0	Percent abroad - English	11.6	Percent tertiary abroad	4.4
Est. tertiary enrollment	103,172	Num. tertiary institutions	37	Students abroad	4,530

HOST	STUDENTS
Belgium	2,684
France	880
United States	411
Germany	206
All others	349

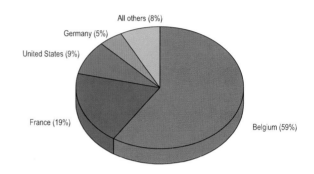

All others (8%)
Germany (5%)
United States (9%)
France (19%)
Belgium (59%)

Uzbekistan

Low Income | **Republic; authoritarian presidential rule** | **Muslim 88%**

Population, 2000 (mil)	24.9	GDP per capita (US$)	2,441	HDI rank	95
Percent in EU	11.2	Percent abroad - English	14.0	Percent tertiary abroad	0.7
Est. tertiary enrollment	681,969	Num. tertiary institutions	23	Students abroad	4,504

HOST	STUDENTS
Russia	3,288
United States	418
Germany	234
United Kingdom	212
Turkey	205
All others	147

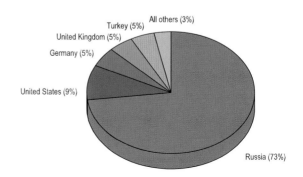

All others (3%)
Turkey (5%)
United Kingdom (5%)
Germany (5%)
United States (9%)
Russia (73%)

			Indigenous beliefs 21%		**Ghana**

Low Income **Constitutional Democracy**

Population, 2000 (mil)	**19.3**	GDP per capita (US$)	**1,964**	HDI rank	**129**
Percent in EU	**36.5**	Percent abroad - English	**84.0**	Percent tertiary abroad	**19.0**
Est. tertiary enrollment	**23,507**	Num. tertiary institutions	**14**	Students abroad	**4,466**

HOST	STUDENTS
United States	2,469
United Kingdom	1,053
Germany	374
All others	570

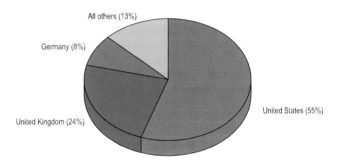

All others (13%)

Germany (8%)

United Kingdom (24%)

United States (55%)

DATA SOURCES AND DEFINITIONS

● **Human Development Index (HDI)**

The HDI is a composite measure of human development, and was created by the United Nations Development Program to convey a sense of the achievements of particular countries in satisfying basic human needs in three areas. The HDI includes a proxy for a long and healthy life, as measured by life expectancy at birth; knowledge, as measured by the adult literacy rate, and primary, secondary and tertiary gross enrollment rates; and a decent standard of living, as measured by gross domestic product per capita. It is not a measure of liberty or global integration. HDI rank is the simple ranking of places by their HDI score.

SOURCE: *Human Development Report 2002* UNDP and http://www.undp.org/

● **Life Expectancy**

The number of years a newborn infant would live if prevailing patterns of age specific mortality rates at the time of birth were to stay the same throughout the child's life.

SOURCE: *Human Development Report 2002* UNDP and http://www.undp.org/

● **Urbanization**

The urban population of a place is expressed as a percent of the total population in 2000, and includes the population of areas defined as urban in each country, as reported to the United Nations.

SOURCE: *Human Development Report 2002* UNDP and http://www.undp.org/

● **Phone Lines**

Telephone mainlines per 1,000 people is defined as a telephone line connecting a subscriber to the telephone exchange equipment, as of 2000. This is the most fundamental measure of the infusion of basic communications technology in a country. It is correlated with other measures such as personal computer use and the number of internet providers.

SOURCE: *Human Development Report 2002* UNDP and http://www.undp.org/

● **Civil Liberties**

Freedom House annually publishes a Freedom in the World report, which rates countries on measures of liberty. Freedom House designates countries with an average score for civil liberties as either free, partly free and not free on a scale of 1 to 7. Elements in the rating include freedom of expression, association, rule of law and personal and economic rights including equality of opportunity.

SOURCE: Freedom House. 2001, *Freedom in the World 2000/2001: The Annual Survey of Political Rights and Civil Liberties.*

● **Press Freedom**

Freedom House's annual press freedom survey covers 192 countries and rates each country's media as "Free," "Partly Free," or "Not Free" on a scale of 0 to 100. Included in the ratings are the legal environments for the media, political pressures that influence reporting, and economic factors that affect access to information.

SOURCE: Freedom House. 2000. *Press Freedom Survey 2000.* http://www.freedomhouse.org/pfs2000. April 2002.

Aircraft Departures

The movement of people between countries by air is associated with economic development and global integration. Air travel also requires a well-developed technological infrastructure that can support civil aviation. As such it can be taken as a proxy measure for the technological basis upon which global integration rests. This data series is for the year 2001.

SOURCE: World Bank Development Indicator database http://www.worldbank.org/data/

Investment

The flow of capital across borders is a primary indicator of a country's integration with the global economy, and is related in many cases to the total number of international students studying abroad. A strong measure of national integration with the global economy is the extent to which other country nationals and organizations invest in a country. Investment is the sum of the absolute value of inflows of foreign direct investment recorded in the balance of payments financial account. It includes equity capital, reinvestment of earnings, other long-term capital, and short-term capital. This data series is for the year 2001.

SOURCE: World Bank Development Indicator database http://www.worldbank.org/data/

Population

Population as of 2000 is the total population, which includes all people actually present in a given area at a given time.

SOURCE: *Human Development Report 2002* UNDP and http://www.undp.org/
For an alternate source see the UN Population Division site:
http://www.un.org/esa/population/unpop.htm

The World Bank Classification of Countries, 2002

The World Bank classifies member economies, and all other economies with populations of more than 30,000 among income groups according to 2001 gross national income (GNI) per capita, calculated using the World Bank Atlas method. The groups are: low income, $745 or less; lower middle-income, $746–2,975; upper middle-income, $2,976–9,205; and high income, $9,206 or more. This scheme is used throughout this atlas to describe the relative economic wealth of a nation or the national origins of students who seek an international education. It is not a measure of the wealth of individuals.

SOURCE: World Bank http://www.worldbank.org

International Students (Students Abroad)

In this atlas a strong effort was made to include data that was readily available either in print or, preferably on the web. In many cases multiple sources for international student data were available. When multiple years were available, use was made of 2000 data. Students abroad refers to students enrolled in host country institutions as reported by those host countries.

Organisation for Economic Co-operation and Development

OECD data includes non-national students if they do not have the citizenship of the country for which the data are reported. However this atlas made use of the data series for those who come to the country expressly for the purpose of pursuing their education ("non-resident foreign students"). http://www.oecd.org

Australia: IDP Education Australia, http://www.idp.com/ and the Australian Government International Education Network, http://aei.detya.gov.au/

Canada: Association of Universities and Colleges of Canada, http://www.aucc.ca

France: ftp://trf.education.gouv.fr/pub/edutel/dpd/rers01/chap6.pdf

Germany: *Wissenschaft Weltoffen 2002* published by the German Academic Exchange Service (DAAD), http://www.wissenschaft-weltoffen.de

Ireland: Higher Education Authority, http://www.hea.ie/

Japan: *Outline of the Student Exchange System in Japan, 2002* published by the Japan Ministry of Education (Monbukagakusho) and http://www.mext.go.jp

New Zealand: New Zealand Vice-Chancellors Committee and *Foreign Fee-Paying Student Statistics to 2001* published by the New Zealand Ministry of Education

Taiwan: *Education in the Republic of China 2002*, published by the Ministry of Education, Republic of China

United Kingdom: British Council, http://www.britishcouncil.org/ and the Higher Education Statistics Agency (HESA), http://www.hesa.ac.uk

United States: *Open Doors* published by the Institute of International Education, http://opendoors.iienetwork.org/

● **Number of Tertiary Institutions**
The number of institutions of higher education by country as listed in the *World Higher Education Database 2000* published by the International Association of Universities.

● **Government Type**
Is taken from the CIA Fact Book, http://www.cia.gov/cia/publications/factbook

● **Primary Religion**
Is taken from the CIA Fact Book, http://www.cia.gov/cia/publications/factbook

● **Estimated Tertiary Enrollment**
This figure is derived from the UNESCO population total for 1997 and the number of higher education students reported to UNESCO in 1996, per 100,000 inhabitants and is taken from the *UNESCO Statistical Yearbook*, and http://www.unesco.org/

In terms of population, 20 percent of the world's population lives in countries that enjoy a free press.

Source: Freedom House

Reflection: With only a small proportion of the world's people exposed to a free press, international education represents a major force for the free exchange of ideas in the world.

CLASSIFICATION OF GEOGRAPHICAL AND POLITICAL REGIONS

Sub-Saharan Africa

Angola
Benin
Botswana
Burkina Faso
Burundi
Cameroon
Cape Verde
Central African Republic
Chad
Comoros
Congo, DPR
Congo, Republic
Côte d'Ivoire
Djibouti
Equatorial Guinea
Ethiopia
Gabon
Gambia
Ghana
Guinea
Guinea-Bissau
Kenya
Lesotho
Liberia
Madagascar
Malawi
Mali
Mauritania
Mauritius
Mozambique
Namibia
Niger
Nigeria
Reunion
Rwanda
São Tomé & Príncipe
Senegal
Seychelles
Sierra Leone
Somalia
South Africa
Swaziland
Tanzania
Togo
Uganda
Zambia
Zimbabwe

North Africa & Middle East

Algeria
Bahrain
Canary Islands
Egypt
Iran
Iraq
Israel
Jordan
Kuwait
Lebanon
Libya
Morocco
Oman
Qatar
Saudi Arabia
Sudan
Syria
Tunisia
United Arab Emirates
Western Sahara
Yemen

East Asia

China
Hong Kong
Japan
Korea, DPR
Korea, Republic of
Macau
Mongolia
Taiwan

South & Central Asia

Afghanistan
Bangladesh
Bhutan
India
Kazakhstan
Kyrgyzstan
Maldives
Nepal
Pakistan
Sri Lanka
Tajikistan
Turkmenistan
Uzbekistan

South East Asia

Brunei
Cambodia
Indonesia
Laos
Malaysia
Myanmar
Philippines
Singapore
Thailand
Vietnam

Latin America & Caribbean

Anguilla
Antigua & Barbuda
Argentina
Aruba
Bahamas
Barbados
Belize
Bolivia
Brazil
British Virgin Islands
Cayman Islands
Chile
Colombia
Costa Rica
Cuba
Dominica
Dominican Republic
Ecuador
El Salvador
Falkland Islands
French Guiana
Grenada
Guadeloupe
Guatemala
Guyana
Haiti
Honduras
Jamaica
Martinique
Mexico
Netherlands
Nicaragua

Panama
Paraguay
Peru
Puerto Rico
St. Kitts & Nevis
St. Lucia
St. Vincent
Suriname
Trinidad & Tobago
Turks & Caicos Islands
Uruguay
Venezuela

North America

Bermuda
Canada
United States

European Union

Austria
Belgium
Denmark
Finland
France
Germany
Greece
Ireland
Italy
Luxembourg
Netherlands
Portugal
Spain
Sweden
United Kingdom

Europa *

Albania
Andorra
Armenia
Azerbaijan
Azores (Portugal)
Belarus
Bosnia & Herzegovina
Bulgaria
Croatia
Cyprus
Czech Republic
Estonia
Georgia
Gibraltar
Greenland
Holy See
Hungary
Iceland
Latvia
Liechtenstein
Lithuania
Macedonia, FYR
Malta
Moldova
Monaco
Norway
Poland
Romania
Russia
San Marino
Serbia & Montenegro
Slovakia
Slovenia
Switzerland
Turkey
Ukraine

Oceania

Australia
Cook Islands
Fiji
French Polynesia
Kiribati
Marshall Islands
Micronesia,
   Federated States
Nauru
New Caledonia
New Zealand
Niue
Palau
Papua New Guinea
Solomon Islands
Tonga
Tuvalu
Vanuatu
Western Samoa

* Europe outside of
   the European Union

ACKNOWLEDGEMENTS

I have wanted to do a project like this for many years. This atlas would still be a dream if it had not been for the vision and support of Jorge Balon and the Ford Foundation. It would have been impossible to sustain a data analytic effort of this magnitude without this fundamental support.

The Institute of International Education remains for me a supportive intellectual home base, and I am indebted to my many colleagues within this fine organization who have worked to make this project a reality.

As is typical of efforts such as this, many others contributed to this project in varied ways. I am especially indebted to Anthony Bohem, with IDP Education Australia and Neil Kemp, with the British Council. Both of these colleagues provided access to data, but most of all were generous with their support and friendship. I like to think that our Anglophonic connections across three continents and two great oceans are one example of the power of liberal globalization.

International mobility of students is a complex and multifaceted phenomenon that has a clear geographic component. Map objects are information dense and perfectly suited to convey the richness and subtlety of the phenomena, but only if the reader pauses to reflect on what this collection of objects has to say. I am indebted to Edward Tufte and Rem Koolhaas for their examples of information design and presentation. Closer to the project, Renée Meyer provided design and graphic support as she worked to take the individual elements of this atlas and weld them into a coherent whole, and Alan Flint, with AGS, who understood that this project's look and feel were tightly bound to its larger purposes. Marie O'Sullivan as always, on time, careful, indispensable. Alison Doorbar, with JWT Education, the project's muse was there when this atlas was just a thought.

Finally, my grandfather, Francis J. Kleban, who taught me how to understand the world and that I had a role to play in it. I wish he were still here – but I know he is always next to me.

In an effort that draws so widely on a variety of data sources, the probability of human error is always present. I take full responsibility for any mistakes that have found their way into the graphic objects or the text.

Todd M. Davis
Senior Scholar
Institute of International Education

New York City
September 2003